The Right Word

THE
RIGHT
WORD

Correcting Commonly Confused,
Misspelled,
and Misused Words

Elizabeth Morrison

CAREER
PRESS
Pompton Plains, NJ

THE RIGHT WORD
EDITED BY JODI BRANDON
TYPESET BY EILEEN MUNSON
Cover design by Howard Grossman
Printed in the U.S.A.

To order this title, please call toll-free 1-800-CAREER-1 (NJ and Canada: 201-848-0310) to order using VISA or MasterCard, or for further information on books from Career Press.

Text Copyright © Elizabeth Morrison
Exisle Publishing Ltd 2012
Published by arrangement with Exisle Publishing Ltd

CAREER
PRESS

The Career Press, Inc.
220 West Parkway, Unit 12
Pompton Plains, NJ 07444
www.careerpress.com

Library of Congress Cataloging-in-Publication Data
Morrison, Elizabeth (Teacher)
  The Right word : correcting commonly confused, misspelled, and misused words / By Elizabeth Morrison.
     pages cm
  Includes bibliographical references and index.
  ISBN 978-1-60163-335-4 -- ISBN 978-1-60163-429-0 (ebook) 1. English language--Usage--Handbooks, manuals, etc. 2. English language--Errors in usage--Handbooks, manuals, etc. 3. English language--Orthography and spelling--Handbooks, manuals, etc. 4. English language--Textbooks for foreign speakers. I. Title.

PE1460M67 2014
428'.1--dc23

                                                        2014009775

\|/

Dedication

*To all teachers
who endeavor tirelessly
to assist students
to understand the complexities
of the English language.*

/|\

ꝫ Acknowledgments ꝫ

This project has taken quite a considerable time, and I would like to thank my husband, Ron, for his unfailing support and enthusiasm, and my family, my friends, and the staffs at Exisle Publishing and Career Press.

⋛ Disclaimer ⋜

Although this book is intended as a general information resource and all care has been taken in compiling the contents, neither the author nor the publisher and their distributors can be held responsible for any loss, claim, or action that may arise from reliance on the information contained in this book.

you

gaff

right

gate

whether

pedal

write

ewe

faint

weather

revue

review

later

disinterested

peddle

feint

emigrant

warn

all

thrown

latter

awl

immigrant

uninterested

mistrust

distrust

CONTENTS

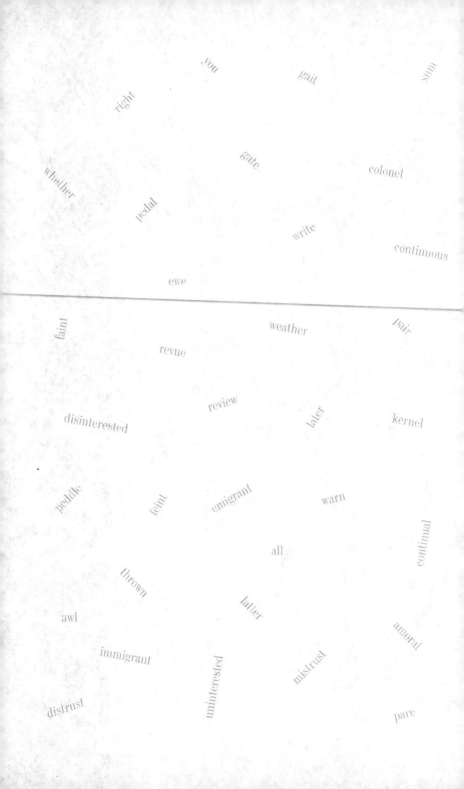

you

gait

sum

right

gate

colonel

whether

pedal

write

continuous

ewe

faint

weather

pair

revue

review

later

kernel

disinterested

peddle

feint

emigrant

warn

all

continual

thrown

latter

awl

amoral

immigrant

uninterested

mistrust

distrust

pare

yon

gait

right

gate

whether

pedal

write

ewe

faint

weather

revue

review

disinterested

hater

peddle

feint

emigrant

warn

all

thrown

latter

awl

immigrant

uninterested

mistrust

distrust

PREFACE

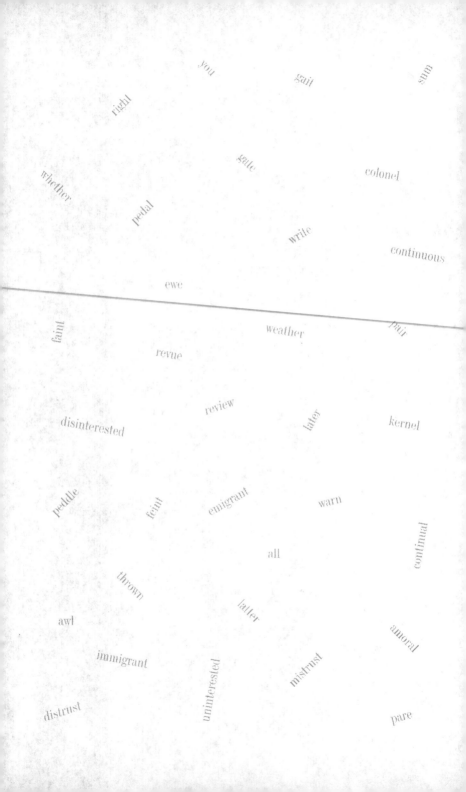

This book was originally designed to assist students (particularly those for whom English was a second language) with the difficulties they encountered when writing. Many of my students studying communications were from non-English-speaking countries.

Problems with English usage became evident when students encountered words that had the same sound but were spelled differently and had different meanings (e.g., cite/sight/site). Spellcheck could not be relied on every time to identify a word spelled incorrectly, particularly if it seemed correct in the context.

These words are known as homophones. (The word *homophone* derives from the Greek *homos*, meaning "same," and *phone*, meaning "sound.")

Searching for the correct spelling of homophones using a dictionary can be quite daunting and time consuming, as many times they appear under different letters of the English alphabet (e.g., knot/not, air/heir, cue/queue, right/rite/write). To overcome this problem, the homophones in this book appear in alphabetical order and all have cross-references to the full entry. (For example, cue/queue appears under C with a cross-reference to Q.) To assist understanding, I have included, in most cases, the correct usage of homophones in phrases or sentences as well as definitions. If a common saying is included, it will be in bold so the reader better understands the term in everyday language.

After I started working on this book, I realized that many of the general population, even if a native speaker, would find it very useful. Certainly many people have difficulty with the correct spelling and usage of words such as principal/principle, stationary/stationery, and their/there/they're. Also, some translators, particularly those writing subtitles for English-speaking audiences or providing technical information for English-speaking customers, should find this book beneficial.

In a separate section, I have included other words that can cause considerable confusion (e.g., elicit/illicit, childish/childlike, imply/infer, and others such as alright/all right, altogether/all together). A list of commonly misspelled words has been added also.

To all who have problems with words that have the same or similar sound or words that can be confused, this guide should be of great benefit.

"Eye am shore ewe knead too reed The Write/Right Word *two rite well."*

Elizabeth Morrison
April 2014

you

gait

right

gate

whether

pedal

write

ewe

weather

faint

revue

review

later

disinterested

peddle

feint

emigrant

warn

all

thrown

latter

awl

immigrant

uninterested

mistrust

distrust

AN A TO Z OF HOMOPHONES

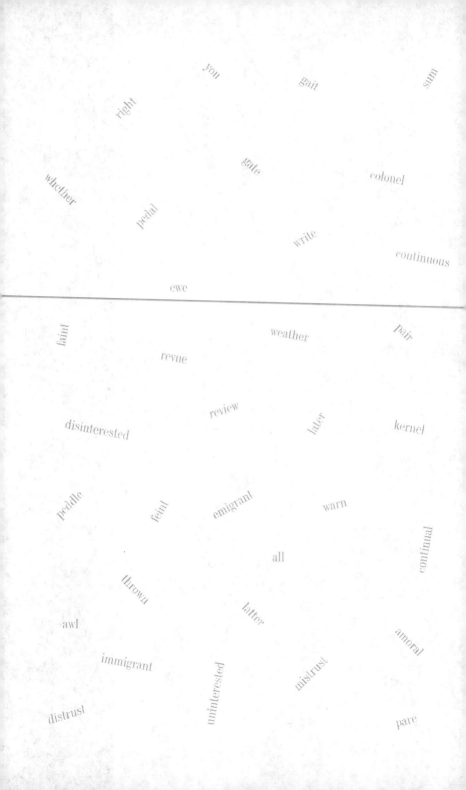

you

gait

sum

right

gale

colonel

whether

pedal

write

continuous

ewe

faint

weather

Pair

revue

review

later

kernel

disinterested

peddle

feint

emigrant

warn

continual

all

thrown

awl

latter

amoral

immigrant

uninterested

mistrust

distrust

pare

⋛ A ⋚

a/A/eh

> **a:** The first letter of the English alphabet (**a**, b, c...); also used before nouns as emphasis (this is **a** beautiful beach; he is **a** prince among people)

> **A:** The first in any series (**A**, B, C, D); a grading mechanism (John received an "**A**" for mathematics); in music, a note and a corresponding scale (one of my favorite pieces of music is Edvard Grieg's "Piano Concerto in **A** Minor")

> **eh:** An expression used to indicate not hearing correctly what was said (**eh**, what did you say?)

A/a/eh (see a/A/eh)

acts/axe

> **Acts:** To indicate performances or actions (his many **acts** of bravery were recognized by a grateful public; she **acts** as a substitute when the star is ill; she **acts** her age) or artistically (there were three **acts** in the play); to describe government rulings (**acts** of Congress)

> **axe:** An implement used to cut wood (he used an **axe** to cut down the tree); to eliminate (they decided to **axe** the television program when the ratings fell)

ad/add

ad: A shortened form of "advertisement" (did you put an **ad** in the newspaper to sell your car?)

add: To increase number, volume, size, or importance (I usually **add** more water to this recipe; I **add** emphasis to this word to increase its effect); or to find the sum of (**add** up both columns of numbers)

add/ad (see ad/add)

adds/ads/adze

adds: Third person singular of "add" (previous entry) (he **adds** up the petty cash every evening)

ads: Plural form of "ad" (previous entry) (several **ads** were placed in the newspaper last Saturday)

adze: A heavy steel tool with a wooden handle used to shape wood

ads/adds/adze (see adds/ads/adze)

adze/ads/adds (see adds/ads/adze)

aerie/airy

aerie: The lofty nest of large birds, such as eagles or hawks

airy: Breezy (it is very **airy** with all the windows open); used also to denote a lightness in appearance or manner, or a flippancy (she has a very **airy** manner)

aid/aide

aid: To help or assist (he came to her **aid** when she fell down; nations give financial **aid** to overcome poverty in Third World countries); to assist with hearing (do you need to wear a hearing **aid** all the time or only through the day?)

aide: An assistant (he was appointed an **aide** to the governor)

aide/aid (see aid/aide)

ail/ale

ail: To feel pain, or be ill or unwell

ale: An alcoholic or soft drink (he drank so much **ale** that he was incapable of driving home; ginger **ale** is a favorite among children)

air/ere/heir

air: What we breathe; the composition of the atmosphere (the world is aiming for clean **air**); used also to indicate appearance (she has a special **air** about her); to overcome tension (to clear the **air**); a melody or tune (Bach composed "**Air** on the G String")

ere: Poetic term meaning "before" (**ere** we meet)

heir: One who inherits (Prince Charles is the **heir** to the British throne)

airy/aerie (see aerie/airy)

aisle/I'll/isle

aisle: A passageway between seats in theaters, churches, aircraft, etc. (the bride walked slowly down the **aisle** of the church on the arm of her father)

I'll: Shortened form of "I will" (**I'll** take you to the circus next Saturday)

isle: A small island (the **Isle** of Pines in the Pacific Ocean is included in the itinerary of many cruises)

ale/ail (see ail/ale)

all/awl

all: Inclusive term meaning everyone or everything (I have packed **all** the clothes I need for the holiday; **all** our favorite programs are shown at night)

awl: A pointed instrument used to pierce holes in leather, wood, etc.; a type of butterfly

allowed/aloud

allowed: Given permission (John was **allowed** to play the piano); to admit or concede (he **allowed** that he had made a mistake in the calculations; in the expenses I have **allowed** for the depreciation on the car)

aloud: To talk loudly (it is irritating when patrons talk **aloud** in movie theaters)

aloud/allowed (see allowed/aloud)

altar/alter

altar: A communion table at the front of a Christian church (churchgoers take communion at the **altar**)

alter: To modify or change (it is common practice to **alter** a digital photographic image)

alter/altar (see altar/alter)

analyst/annalist

analyst: A person who analyzes [e.g., a chemical **analyst**, a political **analyst**, a psycho**analyst,**

annalist: A writer of historical annals or periodical journals of learned institutions

annalist/analyst (see analyst/annalist)

ante/anti

ante: A poker stake (before the deal, the players agree on the initial stake in the pot and put their money on the table, this is known as the **ante**); colloquial: **upped/ upping the ante** is used to indicate an increased offer or extra effort (he **upped the ante** to $10 million to buy the football club; he made a successful takeover bid by **upping the ante**)

anti: against or opposed to (many people were **anti** the war in Iraq)

anti/ante (see ante/anti)

arc/ark

arc: A part of the circumference of a circle; bow-shaped; a luminous bridge between two separate carbon poles (the rainbow formed a perfect **arc**)

ark: The vessel built by Noah during the Great Flood (in the biblical story, Noah took animals two by two onto the **ark**); the **ark** of the covenant, a wooden chest containing tables of Jewish law (the holy **ark** is the most sacred object of Jerusalem)

ark/arc (see arc/ark)

ascent/assent

ascent: To rise; to advance (it takes great courage, skill, and determination to tackle the **ascent** to the top of Mount Everest)

assent: To agree with something (you have my **assent**)

assent/ascent (see ascent/assent)

assistance/assistants

assistance: To give aid (volunteers gave valuable **assistance** during the floods)

assistants: Helpers (many **assistants** were required to help clean up)

assistants/assistance (see assistance/assistants)

ate/eight

ate: Consumed (**I ate** so much cake, I will probably be sick)

eight: A cardinal number as the symbol **8**; depicts this number of items or persons (**eight** people jumped into the surf to save two children caught in the rip)

attendance/attendants

attendance: The people who attend a meeting, function, or event, etc. (no one called in sick, so there was full **attendance** at the office today)

attendants: People who occupy a specific position at an official event [e.g., bridesmaids] (there were many **attendants** at the royal wedding of Prince William and Catherine Middleton)

attendants/attendance (see attendance/attendants)

auger/augur

auger: A spiral tool used for boring holes in wood or an instrument for boring into soil

augur: To foretell, predict; a sign boding either ill or well (all the signs **augur** well for the coming festival)

augur/auger (see auger/augur)

aural/oral

aural: Relating to the ear, or sense of hearing (the doctor ordered an **aural** test to check the patient's range of hearing)

oral: Spoken, verbal (the student gave an **oral** presentation to the class); relating to the mouth (the doctor prescribed an **oral** dose of medicine twice daily)

auricle/oracle

auricle: The outer part of the ear in humans and animals

oracle: A saying, prophecy, or proclamation; a person offering wise counsel or divine prophesies (in Sophocles's play, Oedipus consulted the **oracle** who told him he would kill his father and marry his mother)

away/aweigh

away: Absent (I was **away** from work today); distance (the fire was far **away**); colloquial: meaning not listening or incapable of understanding (**away** with the fairies); sporting events not played on the home field, court, etc. (the team has an **away** game on Saturday)

aweigh: A nautical term (anchors **aweigh**)

aweigh/away (see away/aweigh)

awl/all (see all/awl)

axe/acts (see acts/axe)

axel/axle

axel: An ice-skating term referring to a jump with one-and-a-half turns (or more) in the air from one skate to the other (the spectators clapped when the ice skater performed a triple **axel** during her performance)

axle: The shaft, pin, bar, or similar that is used to rotate a wheel or pair of wheels (farmer Jones was annoyed when the **axle** broke on his cart and the wheel fell off)

axes/axis

axes: The plural of "axe" (the men used their **axes** with great dexterity in the wood-chopping event at the agricultural show)

axis: A real or imaginary line about which a body, such as the earth, rotates; an alliance or agreement of two or more powers to coordinate their foreign and military policies (during World War II, Germany, Italy, and Japan were referred to as the **Axis** powers)

axis/axes (see axes/axis)

axle/axel (see axel/axle)

aye/eye/I

aye: Used as an alternative to "yes" (the **ayes** have the majority); a nautical expression (**aye**, **aye**, Captain)

eye: The organ of sight (some people have one blue and one green **eye**); to observe, glance, or watch (the warden kept an **eye** on the prisoner); to be fond of someone (she was the **apple of my eye**); to ignore (the pedestrian turned **a blind eye** to the car accident); to be discerning or a good judge of something (he has a good **eye** for interior design); used also in conjunction with superstition (she has the evil **eye**) or desire (she has her **eye** on that dress)

I: Personal pronoun (**I** wish **I** could win the lottery)

ꗳ B ꗳ

B/be/bee

B: The second letter in the English alphabet; the second in any series (A, **B**, C, D); a grade (Jo received a "**B**" in English); in music, a major or minor chord (Franz Liszt composed the "Piano Sonata in **B** Minor" in 1854)

be: Part of the auxiliary verb "to be" (I want to **be** a great writer; how can you **be** so calm?; from Shakespeare's *Hamlet*, "To **be**, or not to **be**, that is the question")

bee: A hive insect that makes a buzzing sound and produces wax and honey (the most important **bee** in the hive is the female queen **bee**); colloquial: someone who is admired (she is the **bee's knees**); also used to indicate a busy group of people (a working **bee**); a contest (a spelling **bee**); to indicate an obsession (she has a **bee in her bonnet**)

baa/bah

baa: The bleating sound made by a sheep (***Baa Baa Black Sheep*** is a well-known nursery rhyme)

bah: An exclamation of contempt or disgust (**bah,** you don't know what you are talking about!)

bade/bayed

bade: Past tense of "to bid," meaning to order or request (I **bade** her not to make those rude noises)

bayed: A bark made by large dogs, particularly hounds (the dog **bayed** at the moon)

bah/baa (see baa/bah)

bail/bale

bail: The security given to release a prisoner into custody of another person (his **bail** was set at the maximum amount; **bail** was denied, as the prisoner was considered a risk to the community); to help or assist, particularly financially (his father was able to secure the finance to **bail** out his son from his gambling debts); the action of scooping water (his job was to **bail** out the water if the boat started to leak)

bale: A large bundle usually for storage or transportation (a **bale** of hay)

baited/bated

baited: Using poisoned food to kill animals (Kim cried for days when her dog ate the **baited** food and died); to place food on a hook to catch fish (Ron **baited** his hooks with worms to catch flathead); to use inflammatory or insulting words to anger (the drunken louts **baited** people walking past with rude gestures and swear words)

bated: To restrain (he waited with **bated** breath to hear the results); to moderate (he experienced many setbacks that **bated** his hopes of advancement in the company)

bald/balled/bawled

bald: Hairless (he wore a wig to conceal he was **bald**); having little or no tread (he was pulled over by the police for having **bald** tires)

balled: Squeezed or molded into a rounded shape (he **balled** up his dirty clothes); also appears in the expression **blackballed,** meaning a negative vote that excludes membership (his reputation had preceded him and when he applied for membership of the club he was **blackballed**)

bawled: Past tense of "to bawl," meaning to cry loudly (she **bawled** when she fell down the stairs)

bale/bail (see bail/bale)

ball/bawl

ball: A round or spherical body such as a sphere or a globe (a **ball** can take many shapes [e.g., footballs and tennis balls]); a formal dance (the mayoral **ball** was an important event)

bawl: To cry loudly (I shudder whenever I hear my baby **bawl**, fearing he might be hurt)

balled/bawled/bald (see bald/balled/bawled)

band/banned

band: A group of persons with a common purpose (they **band** together to raise money for cancer research; a musical **band**); radio frequencies (a **band** is defined between two distinct frequency limits)

banned: Prohibited or limited by law (underage teenagers are **banned** from attending this event; alcohol is **banned** in this area)

banned/band (see band/banned)

bard/barred

bard: A Celtic minstrel or poet (Shakespeare is the best-known **bard**)

barred: Forbidden or excluded (he was **barred** from attending the celebrations)

bare/bear

bare: Unclothed, naked (his chest was **bare** and completely hairless); unadorned, plain (her neck was **bare** without any jewelry; the **bare** facts were given in evidence)

bear: An animal (a grizzly **bear** is known to be very dangerous); to carry or support (he had to **bear** the weight of the load on his shoulders); to suffer (she will **bear** the pain of the loss all her life); to produce (many trees **bear** fruit)

baron/barren

baron: A peerage, a title (**barons** in England are lower in status than princes, dukes, and lords); a very powerful or rich man, a magnate (American "robber **barons**" were regarded as unscrupulous)

barren: Not capable of reproducing (because she was **barren**, she was unable to have children; the land was **barren**) barred/bard (see bard/barred)

barren/baron (see baron/barren)

base/bass

base: The bottom (the **base** of the vase was cracked); low, cowardly (it was a **base** action to steal from the old woman)

bass: A deep sound, particularly referring to music (he was a **bass** singer in the church choir)

based/baste

based: To be located at a particular place (Josh is **based** at the army camp at Holsworthy, New South Wales)

baste: To sew or tack with large temporary stitches in the first stages of making a garment (Beryl's practice was to **baste** the sides and shoulders of a jacket to have a fitting before completing the garment); to moisten meat with liquid during cooking (when baking a leg of lamb, the cook would **baste** the leg several times during the cooking time)

bask/Basque

bask: To lie in the sun or warmth (to **bask** in the sunshine; to **bask** in the attention given)

Basque: An autonomous region in northern Spain (the **Basque** refers to people of this region and also many who live in France and the Pyrenees)

Basque/bask (see bask/Basque)

bass/base (see base/bass)

baste/based (see based/baste)

bat/batt

> **bat:** A nocturnal animal with webbed wings that eats mainly fruit or insects; colloquial: to have poor vision (she is as **blind as a bat**); an implement used in sport to strike a ball [e.g., baseball **bat**]

> **batt:** Material used to insulate buildings; cottonwool filling in quilts

bated/baited (see baited/bated)

batt/bat (see bat/batt)

bawl/ball (see ball/bawl)

bawled/bald/balled (see bald/balled/bawled)

bayed/bade (see bade/bayed)

bazaar/bizarre

> **bazaar:** A marketplace where goods are sold often in stalls, particularly in Egypt, Turkey, and Asia (tourists particularly like visiting **bazaars** to buy souvenirs); the sale of assorted items to raise funds [e.g., church **bazaar**]

> **bizarre:** Odd, eccentric, unusual (the clothes she wears are quite **bizarre**)

be/bee/B (see B/be/bee)

beach/beech

beach: Sand and/or sea pebbles between the sea and the shoreline (our greatest pleasure was building sandcastles on the **beach**); to run a boat onto the shore (it was necessary to **beach** our boat)

beech: A tree grown in temperate regions that has smooth, gray bark

bear/bare (see bare/bear)

beat/beet

beat: To hit or strike repeatedly (the assailant **beat** him almost to death); to win a race (the second-favorite horse **beat** last year's winner); to mark out a specific area (the policeman's **beat** was around Piccadilly Circus)

beet: A plant with succulent roots (best-known **beets** are the **beetroot** and the white **beet**, used to produce sugar)

beau/bow

beau: A lover, sweetheart, escort (is your **beau** taking you to the ball?)

bow: A flexible piece of wood easily bent and used to shoot arrows (Robin Hood is well known for his prowess with the **bow**); a rod with horsehair used to play the violin; colloquial: to have more than one resource (he has more than two strings to his **bow**)

bee/B/be (see B/be/bee)

beech/beach (see beach/beech)

beer/bier

beer: An alcoholic beverage fermented and brewed from a malted grain and flavored with hops (once an alcoholic drink for mainly men in pubs, today **beer** is a favorite among both men and women); also a non-alcoholic drink [e.g., ginger **beer**]

bier: A moveable stand on which a coffin or corpse can be placed and taken to the grave (the mourners followed the **bier** to the cemetery for the burial service)

beet/beat (see beat/beet)

bell/belle

bell: A hollow piece of metal with a flared mouth that emits a noise when struck (the school **bell** rings when classes are to begin); an instrument that emits a continuous ringing noise (the door **bell** ringing at night is often a sign of bad news); also used at sea to denote the half-hour period of watch (Tom hated being on first watch, as the ship's **bell** is rung at 0300 hours and then every half hour to announce the time of day)

belle: A girl or woman admired for her beauty (she was the **belle** of the ball)

belle/bell (see bell/belle)

berry/bury

berry: A small fruit, such as the strawberry, raspberry, or gooseberry (a straw**berry** is always best when eaten fresh)

bury: To place in a grave; to become rapt or involved (to **bury** one's head in a book; to **bury** himself in his work); to sink deep (to **bury** a knife in his heart); reconciliation (to **bury** the hatchet)

berth/birth

berth: A sleeping place on either a train or a ship (we booked a two-**berth** cabin); a designated place for a boat to moor (we secured a **berth** at the new marina); colloquial: to avoid (I gave her a wide **berth**)

birth: The arrival of an infant (the **birth** notice for the baby was in the newspaper; we always send a card on his **birth**day); the beginning or origin (he gave **birth** to a brilliant idea to make money)

bi/buy/by/bye

bi: Prefix meaning "two" (the magazine is published **bi**annually; he is **bi**sexual; she wears **bi**focal glasses)

buy: To purchase by paying money (he wants to **buy** a new coat); to stall (she wants to **buy** time); to obtain shares (to **buy** into); colloquial: to get a piece of (to **buy** into an argument)

by: Near to or at the side of (the park is **by** the highway); as a means of conveyance (she came **by** taxi); at a certain time (he said he would arrive **by** 6 p.m.)

bye: A shortened form of "goodbye" (**bye** I will see you tomorrow); in sport when a team doesn't play (the rugby team had a **bye** this week)

bier/beer (see beer/bier)

bight/bite/byte

bight: An inward curve of a coast (the Great Australian **Bight** is a well-known landmark); the section of rope between the ends (he tied the boat with a **bight** of rope)

bite: To cut into with the teeth (he took a large **bite** out of the apple); pungency or a strong flavor (the cheese has a real **bite** to it); colloquial: to attempt something beyond one's ability (he attempted to **bite off more than he could chew**); to be ungrateful (to **bite the hand that feeds you**)

byte: Information stored on a computer

billed/build

billed: Past tense of "to bill," meaning an account of money owed (the contractor **billed** me for services rendered)

build: To construct, erect (the plan was to **build** the house on the edge of the lake); to increase (to **build** the business up)

birth/berth (see berth/birth)

bite/byte/bight (see bight/bite/byte)

bizarre/bazaar (see bazaar/bizarre)

blew/blue

blew: Past tense of the verb "to blow," meaning to move air (he **blew** the bugle at every Memorial Day ceremony; she **blew** bubbles in the soapy water)

blue: A color in the spectrum between green and violet (she wore a **blue** dress); colloquial: to feel down or depressed (she felt **blue** when her boyfriend didn't call); to be out of tune or make a mistake (he played a **blue** note; to occur rarely (once in a **blue moon**)

bloc/block

bloc: A group of states or countries uniting to support a particular view or interest (the Eastern **bloc**); a voting party (the Independents voted as a **bloc**); a trading faction (the suppliers as a **bloc** quoted the same price to all potential buyers)

block: A piece of wood, a tree stump; colloquial: to refer to kinship similarity (he is **a chip off the old block**); a group of housing units (a **block** of apartments); to stop an action (to **block** the merger); a spectacular film (a **block**buster); medically to stop pain (to **block** a nerve)

block/bloc (see bloc/block)

blue/blew (see blew/blue)

boar/boor/bore

boar: A wild male pig

boor: An uncouth, unmannerly person (at parties everyone attempts to avoid John, as he is such a **boor**, drinking to excess and talking in a loud voice)

bore: To drill a hole; to attack violently (he **bore** into him with great vehemence); a person who talks monotonously (everyone avoided him as he was such a **bore**)

board/bored

board: A piece of timber of much longer length than width (veneered wood floor**boards** have replaced carpets in many homes); used in schools (the traditional black**board** has been replaced by electronic boards in many schools); lodging that offers both food and a bed (many people prefer to **board** instead of paying for a hotel); a school that offers accommodation (many parents send their children to **boarding** schools)

bored: To become uninterested or inattentive (he was so long winded I became very **bored**; colloquial: the topic was so uninteresting I was **bored to death**); the act of boring a hole in wood or the earth (the company **bored** a hole in the ground to test for oil)

boarder/border

boarder: A lodger who pays for food and a bed (the landlady advertised for a **boarder**; the school had both day students and **boarders**)

border: A margin or an edge (a **border** around a set of figures makes them stand out); on the edge (he is on the **border** of committing suicide); to adjoin another country (in Europe most countries **border** other regions; you need a passport to cross the **border** into a different country)

bold/bowled

bold: Not hesitating to take action even if considered foolhardy (it was a **bold** plan to capture the fort); overstepping conventions (he was **bold** in his approach to the new president); a description of writing (his written work was **bold** both in style and content); a dark type used in computing and printing (the headlines were in **bold**)

bowled: Colloquial: to make an impression (he **bowled** the new girl over with his charm)

bolder/boulder

bolder: A comparative form of bold (he was **bolder** than all the other boys)

boulder: A large separate rock (they removed the **boulder** from the road to allow traffic to pass)

boor/bore/boar (see boar/boor/bore)

border/boarder (see boarder/border)

bore/boar/boor (see boar/boor/bore)

bored/board (see board/bored)

born/borne

born: To be brought into life (he was **born** on December 8); to originate (the idea was **born** for a satirical revue after viewing the political fiasco)

borne: Past tense of "to bear" (the weight of the decision was **borne** by the whole family)

borne/born (see born/borne)

bough/bow

bough: A large branch of a tree (he climbed the **bough** to reach the apples)

bow: To bend in reverence or respect (you must **bow** when you greet the queen); to submit (**bow** to the inevitable; **bow** your head in shame); to accept a compliment or applause (take a **bow**)

boulder/bolder (see bolder/boulder)

bow/beau (see beau/bow)

bow/bough (see bough/bow)

bowled/bold (see bold/bowled)

braid/brayed

braid: To weave together, intertwine, or plait hair, flowers, silk, etc. (Helen wore her hair plaited in one long **braid** that reached to her waist)

brayed: The past tense of "bray"

braise/brays/braze

braise: A method of stewing and tenderizing meat or vegetables by browning in fat and then slowly cooking in a small amount of liquid

brays: Present tense of "bray" (it is quite noisy when you are visiting a farm and a donkey **brays**); or in plural form (the **brays** of the protesting crowds at the public forum were ear shattering)

braze: To form, fix, or join by soldering with an alloy of copper and zinc at high temperature (it takes practice and skill to be able to **braze** successfully)

brake/break

brake: A device for stopping or slowing a vehicle (you need to **brake** when you approach the bend); also a thicket, a place overgrown with bushes

break: To shatter (be careful or you will **break** the plates); to fail to observe the law or regulations (you will **break** the law if you park there; if you do not wear your medals, you will **break** with tradition); to be the first with a news story (to **break** the news of the winner of the World Cup); to make a discovery (a **break**through in the research into bowel cancer); colloquial: to overcome (females have begun to **break** through the glass ceiling); to have an emotional, psychological, or physical reaction (the long-distance runner suffered a **break**down just before the end of the race; she had a nervous **break**down); to unlawfully enter a property (to **break and enter**); a billiards term (to make a **break**); to escape (to **break out** of prison); to tame (it took time to **break** the horse); colloquial: to take a rest, have a holiday (I have been working too hard and need to take a **break**)

brayed/braid (see braid/brayed)

brays/braze/braise (see braise/brays/braze)

braze/braise/brays (see braise/brays/braze)

breach/breech

breach: To break or rupture (there is a **breach** in relations between the two families); to make a hole in or to break through (the whale leaped out of the water in a spectacular **breach**); to break a contract (she sued him for **breach** of contract)

breech: The birth of a baby bottom first instead of head first (he was a **breech** birth); the lower part of the body known as the buttocks (breeches, an older form of knee-length trousers, came from the word **breech**)

bread/bred

bread: Staple food made into loaves using flour and water with or without yeast and baked (we had two slices of **bread** with tomato and cheese for lunch); colloquial: to know what is in your best interests (to know on which side your **bread** is buttered); the person who earns the money (John is the **bread**winner in our family)

bred: To produce offspring, babies, or animals (the foal was **bred** from two champions)

break/brake (see brake/break)

bred/bread (see bread/bred)

breech/breach (see breach/breech)

brewed/brood

brewed: The past tense of "brews"

brood: A number of young children or animals cared for by one mother (many pitied the mother taking her **brood** of young children with her to shop); birds hatched at the one time; also a verb meaning to dwell on or think deeply about something that has happened or is likely to happen (Harriet often would **brood** about her chances of every marrying)

brews/bruise

brews: Makes beer, ales, by fermenting malt, hops, etc. (the breweries in Tasmania are famous for the pure water used in their **brews**); letting tea stand before pouring (she **brews** the tea for at least two minutes)

bruise: A discoloration of the skin after being hurt (she fell from her scooter and had a **bruise** on her knee); colloquial: to hurt (it didn't take much to **bruise** his feelings)

bridal/bridle

bridal: Related to weddings (she had the most beautiful **bridal** gown; the **bridal** suite was booked months ahead)

bridle: Part of the harness on a horse around the head (the **bridle** on the horse needed to be adjusted); a restraint (she needs to **bridle** her temper); an act of resentment (she was prone to **bridle** when she was criticized)

bridle/bridal (see bridal/bridle)

broach/brooch

broach: A spit for roasting meat; to veer a ship broadside to the wind and waves (the captain saw the large wave approaching and ordered his crew to **broach** the ship to avoid the impact); to introduce a subject for the first time (he decided to **broach** the possibility of a vacation abroad with his wife)

brooch: An ornament with a pin at the back for attaching to a jacket or scarf (Ruth was very proud of the beautiful silver **brooch** left to her by her grandmother in her will)

brooch/broach (see broach/brooch)

brood/brewed (see brewed/brood)

brows/browse

brows: The ridges and hair over the eyes (Veronica had beautiful, arched **brows** that enhanced her beauty); colloquial: to indicate uncertainty or anger (he would often **knit his brows** when he was trying to work out a clue in a crossword puzzle); in singular form, the edge of a steep place (he reached the **brow** of the hill after climbing uphill for 30 minutes)

browse: To graze on pasture (the deer often would **browse** on the field); to read leisurely and casually (it was Elsa's dream to have time to **browse** through the newspaper without interruption); to look casually when shopping (she would often just **browse** through the shops to see what the next season's fashions would be)

browse/brows (see brows/browse)

bruise/brews (see brews/bruise)

build/billed (see billed/build)

bury/berry (see berry/bury)

but/butt

but: Used to indicate an exception or a contrary position (everyone **but** Harry went to the movies; she wanted the car **but** I wouldn't budge); only (there is no one **but** Shirley able to take the position)

butt: The end, usually the thicker part (the **butt** of the rifle); the receiver (he was the **butt** of their jokes); to attack or strike (beware of the goat, he will **butt** you); colloquial: particularly American, referring to the buttocks (I will whip your **butt**); also, to not interfere (I told you to **butt** out)

butt/but (see but/butt)

buy/by/bye/bi (see bi/buy/by/bye)

by/bye/bi/buy (see bi/buy/by/bye)

bye/bi/buy/bi (see bi/buy/by/bye)

byte/bight/bite (see bight/bite/byte)

≳ C ≲

C/sea/see

C: The third letter in the English alphabet; the third in any series (A, B, **C**, D); a grade (you have received a "**C**" for your essay); music (this piece is played in **C** minor)

sea: A vast expanse of salt water (many cruise ships sail the Mediterranean **Sea**); a large wave or swell (a heavy **sea** was responsible for the race being cancelled); to travel by boat (I went by **sea** to England); metaphorically, describing a crowd (all I could see was a **sea** of faces); colloquial: to be confused (Jennifer was **all at sea** when asked what the most popular actors of the 20th century were); colloquial: to change how you live and move from the city to be near to the sea (they decided to make a **sea change** and leave the noise of the city)

see: To perceive, to be aware of (I can **see** you hiding in the bushes; I can **see** the mountains from here); to imagine or to remember (I used to **see** ghosts in my room when I was a child; I can still **see** how you looked when I first met you); to perceive mentally (do you **see** what I was talking about?); to meet informally (I'll **see** you next week); to accompany (I will **see** you home safely); the position or district under control of a bishop or archbishop [e.g., the **see** of Canterbury]

cache/cash

cache: A hiding place to store food, money, etc. (John left a **cache** of money under the floorboards); storage of food by animals over the winter (the bears left a **cache** of nuts as provisions for the long winter months)

cash: Money, either in coins or notes (I needed **cash** to put into the meter); to liquidate an insurance policy or shares (he needed to **cash** in his BHP shares to pay for a new car); to hand in one's counters when gambling (she decided to **cash** in her roulette chips while she was winning); colloquial: to die (poor old John, he has **cashed in his chips**)

callous/callus

callous: To be emotionally hard or unfeeling (he was regarded as a **callous** monster when he drowned the puppies)

callus: A hardened lump of skin (his hands had many a **callus** after years as a laborer)

callus/callous (see callous/callus)

cannon/canon

cannon: An ancient large gun that shot cannonballs and was mounted on a carriage (although usually used in war, shooting a man from a **cannon** was sometimes an entertainment feature in carnivals; colloquial: infantry soldiers charging in open country being fired on by artillery were regarded as **cannon** fodder)

canon: An ecclesiastical decree or a law of the church; a portion of a Mass service; a musical term referring to a piece of music where the tune is repeatedly imitated by different parts; a typeface (the Canon camera logo incorporates the **Canon** font)

canon/cannon (see cannon/canon)

canter/cantor

canter: The easy stride of a horse somewhere between a trot and a gallop (Jane liked to **canter** on her horse but never galloped)

cantor: A church officer who leads the singing in a cathedral or church cantor/canter (see canter/cantor)

canvas/canvass

> **canvas:** A heavy cloth of flax, hemp, or similar material used to make sails or tents (Ben was so angry when the **canvas** split and the rain came into his tent); material on which an oil painting is made (famous oil paintings on **canvas** by van Gogh, Rembrandt, etc. appear in galleries)
>
> **canvass:** To solicit political support, votes, opinions, ideas (the liberal candidate decided to **canvass** for support by going door to door in her district; the manager's practice is to **canvass** for ideas when marketing a new product)

canvass/canvas (see canvas/canvass)

capital/capitol

> **capital:** A city that is the seat of government in a country or state (Paris is the **capital** of France); a capital letter [e.g., B or D] (sentences begin with a **capital** letter); the amount of wealth, property, etc. owned by a person or business (he invested a large amount of **capital** into buying the shopping center); indication of approval (that was a **capital** effort)
>
> **capitol:** Originally a citadel on top of a hill but now specifically refers to the building occupied by the U.S. Congress (**Capitol** Hill is the area in Washington, D.C. where Congress is located)

capitol/capital (see capital/capitol)

carat/caret/carrot

carat: A unit of weight of gemstones, also the fineness of pure gold (Judy displayed her 24-**carat**-gold necklace to all her friends)

caret: An insertion mark indicating that a letter or word has been omitted

carrot: An orange root vegetable (Ken always asked for shredded **carrot** in his salad); colloquial: an incentive (she **dangled a carrot** in front of his nose offering an outing to the movies if he mowed the lawn)

caret/carrot/carat (see carat/caret/carrot)

carol/carrel

carol: A song, particularly a Christmas song or hymn (my favorite **carol** is "Hark! The Herald Angels Sing")

carrel: A small, enclosed place in a university library for students to study (at some colleges and universities, **carrels** are reserved for PhD students)

carrel/carol (see carol/carrel)

carrot/carat/caret (see carat/caret/carrot)

cash/cache (see cache/cash)

cast/caste

cast: The action of throwing (to **cast** a line into the river); to direct (to **cast** a glance over the opposition); to produce (to **cast** a shadow; metal workers pour iron into a mold to **cast** an object); actors in a play or film (often a Cecil B. DeMille movie had a **cast** of thousands); to deposit (we **cast** our votes on the weekend)

caste: Societal groupings based on religion or occupation (India has a rigid **caste** system)

caste/cast (see cast/caste)

cay/key/quay

cay: A small low island with mainly white sand and coral (Musha **Cay** is the most exclusive private resort in the Bahamas)

key: An opener of a lock in a door or gate (he had a habit of forgetting where he left the front door **key**); used to start the engine of a car or machine (very early cars did not have a **key** to start the engine, because you had to pull a knob); indication of importance (he was asked to present the **key** address at the conference); a solution (it is commonly believed that the **key** to success is to work hard and effectively)

quay: A wharf that allows ships to berth (the *Queen Elizabeth* arrived at Circular **Quay** in Sydney last month)

cede/seed

cede: To hand over control to another (she was forced to **cede** control of the company to her son); to hand over territory under a treaty (at the end of the war, the country was forced to **cede** large areas of fertile land in reparations)

seed: Part of a plant that is used to grow new ones (Joan was able to **seed** the ground each year to produce prize-winning flowers); to indicate the beginning (the **seed** of an idea for a new revue was put to the cast members); to rank players in a sport (the committee decided to **seed** Roger Federer number 1 in the U.S. Open tennis tournament)

ceiling/sealing

ceiling: The overhead portion of a room (she wanted the **ceiling** in her bedroom to be painted white); used to indicate a barrier (Jan broke through the glass **ceiling** when she became the new chief executive officer)

sealing: The act of completion (he proposed **sealing** the deal with a handshake); completing an official document with an imprinted stamp or symbol (**sealing** a document with an imprinted stamp shows its importance)

cell/sell

cell: A confined space or small room (the prisoner was forced to share his **cell** with three other inmates); a group of people combined for a subversive purpose [e.g., terrorist **cell**]; a biological term (we have many **cells** in our body); an electrical term (car batteries have four or six **cells**)

sell: To trade (if I reduce the price, I should **sell** the house this weekend); to promote (I'm sure I can **sell** this idea for a new book to my publishers)

cellar/seller

cellar: An underground room to store items such as wine or coal (a visit to France usually includes a tour of at least one famous underground wine **cellar**); can also refer to a collection of wine

seller: One who trades in goods (he has been a **seller** at the markets since he was a young boy)

censer/censor/sensor

censer: A vessel to burn incense

censor: A person who deems words, books, or films as immoral or offensive (some books axed originally by a **censor** are now regarded as classics, such as *Lady Chatterley's Lover*); removing words that could be regarded as against the nation's interest (it defies freedom of information to **censor** documents from a country's citizens)

sensor: An electrical device that has been devised to sense when something is not right (a **sensor** will detect when there has been an electrical surge or when drugs have been carried in a suitcase)

censor/sensor/censer (see censer/censor/sensor)

cent/scent/sent

cent: A decimal currency coin; colloquial: to indicate being short of money (I haven't got a **cent** to my name)

scent: A perfume (you can choose a **scent** that is either eau de cologne or eau de parfum depending on how much you have to spend); a smell that exudes from an animal (the hounds follow the **scent** of the fox); also colloquial: to be suspicious (there is an unpleasant **scent** about this deal)

sent: To forward on or dispatch (I **sent** you a letter of resignation; I **sent** Sue a bunch of roses for her birthday)

cents/scents/sense

cents: Coins of decimal currency

scents: Plural form of "scent" (there were so many **scents**, the dogs were unsuccessful in following the trail)

sense: To feel (I **sense** that many of the board were not happy with my explanation; I have a sixth **sense** about this situation)

cereal/serial

cereal: An edible grain such as wheat, rye, corn, etc.; breakfast food (her favorite **cereal** is Corn Flakes)

serial: A story published in installments, usually in a magazine or newspaper, or on television (Helen couldn't wait to read the next installment of the **serial** in the paper); also used to describe a criminal who commits the same crime repeatedly (Jack the Ripper was a **serial** killer)

cession/session

cession: The act of giving something up by treaty or by law (after the war the **cession** of lands under the treaty to the victorious nation created many problems, leading to further tensions)

session: A period of time (the afternoon **session** at the movies begins at 2:30 p.m.; they had a **session** with the marriage counselor)

chance/chants

chance: The way events can happen without any valid reason (it was only by **chance** that I took a different path and missed being hit by the car); luck or fortune (I bought the winning lottery ticket by **chance**); to take a risk (Frank took a **chance** when he hired the inexperienced girl)

chants: Songs or singing, particularly religious (you can sometimes hear the monks' **chants**)

chants/chance (see chance/chants)

chased/chaste

chased: Past tense of "to chase": to run after, or drive away (the dog **chased** the cat around the garden; Adam **chased** after the man who stole his wallet); used in sport to attempt to surpass an opponent's score (the score was 1–0 and the opposing team **chased** hard to finally win)

chaste: Pure, virtuous, usually refers to a young woman who has high morals and has never had sexual intercourse

chaste/chased (see chased/chaste)

cheap/cheep

cheap: Not expensive (it was a **cheap** car, less than $10,000); sometimes used to denote an inferior product, often expressed as "**cheap** and nasty" (I should have realized it was too **cheap**; it only lasted a few days before it broke down); colloquial: to have low morals (her clothes made her look so **cheap**)

cheep: A high-pitched, short sound from a young bird

check/Czech

check: To look over to ensure everything is correct (I need to **check** the figures again before I present them to the committee); to restrain (she had to **check** him from hitting his young brother); a pattern of crossed lines forming squares used in material, particularly in tablecloths and dresses (everyone admired her pink and gray **check** dress); a term used in chess (John was thrilled when he said, "**Check**mate" to his opponent); to register at a hotel (we had to **check in** at the hotel by 5 p.m.); to vacate a room at a hotel (we had to **check out** of our room by 11 a.m.)

Czech: A citizen of the Czech Republic or someone who was born there (many **Czechs** have migrated to other countries)

cheep/cheap (see cheap/cheep)

chews/choose

chews: The third person singular of "chew," meaning to masticate or crush and grind food with your teeth (it sickens me when Jake **chews** his food with his mouth open); also used to indicate when a person keeps thinking or worrying about something (he always **chews** it over in his mind before making a decision)

choose: To select (should I **choose** the red or black dress?); to make a decision (I will **choose** which subjects I will study at college)

Chile/chili/chilly

Chile: A country in South America (the pronunciation of **Chile** can vary in different countries)

chili: A hot, pungent fruit of some capsicums (peppers) often used in Indian, Thai, or Vietnamese food (Zac regretted eating the red **chili** in his curry); a dish made from ground beef, chili peppers and/or chili powder, and beans

chilly: Cold but not freezing (it was a **chilly** morning before the sun appeared); also used to refer to a person's manner (she had a **chilly** demeanor)

chili/chilly/Chile (see Chile/chili/chilly)

Chile/chili/chilly (see Chile/chili/chilly)

choir/quire

choir: A group of people who sing together (the Vienna Boys' **Choir** tours the world)

quire: A quantity of paper equal to 1/20th of a ream

choose/chews (see chews/choose)

choral/coral

choral: A piece of music performed by a choir (the **choral** piece chosen was suitable for the occasion)

coral: The skeletons of marine animals that have become hard and limey and formed into reefs (the Great Barrier Reef off the coast of Queensland in northern Australia is a famous **coral** reef)

chord/cord/cored

chord: In music, a number of notes played together (young music students sometimes have difficulty learning the different **chords**); also used when a person remembers something or feels attuned to what another person is saying (what he said **struck a chord** with me)

cord: Similar to string mainly used in blinds, curtains, and pajamas (Jill, you need to tie a knot on the end of the **cord** or your pajama pants will slip)

cored: To take out the center of fruit (Polly needs to **core** and slice the apples before baking them in a pie)

chute/shoot

chute: A slide or channel sloping down that allows grain, water, coal, etc. to descend (a laundry **chute** is very useful to send dirty clothes downstairs to be washed); an abbreviation for "parachute"

shoot: To fire a gun (we were upset when we saw the man **shoot** the kangaroo); to propel a ball toward the net/goal in basketball, soccer, etc. (Stuart, a midfielder, kicked the ball to the striker for him to **shoot** for the goal); colloquial: to make an error (to **shoot himself in the foot**) or to inject drugs (Jill would **shoot up** when she needed heroin)

cite/sight/site

cite: Referring to a statement or quotation (you need to **cite** the references you used in your essay)

sight: The ability to see (the eye specialist said I had perfect **sight**; I caught **sight** of him when he was in the jewelry shop); used as a description (the earthquake damage was a sad **sight**); used colloquially (the plane arriving to rescue survivors was a **sight** for sore eyes); used detrimentally (she was an absolute **sight**)

site: Where a place is located (the **site** of the original settlement is hard to locate)

clause/claws

clause: A grammatical term meaning part of a complex sentence containing its own verb (there are two **clauses** in the sentence "As the swimming pool was closed yesterday, we went to the beach"); part of a contract, legal document, etc. (the money I was entitled to receive was in the second **clause** of the contract)

claws: The pointed nails of animals, birds (the eagle's **claws** assist it to hold its prey); the pincers of shellfish and insects (many people love to eat the flesh in the lobster's **claws**); the divided head of a hammer used to grip and pull out nails (he got exasperated when the nails got caught in the **claws** of the hammer)

claws/clause (see clause/claws)

close/clothes

close: To shut (please **close** the door); to end or finalize (you need to **close** the ballot at the stated time)

clothes: Garments you wear (your **clothes** are a reflection of your personality); a description of a line on which to hang laundry to dry [e.g., **clothes**line]; can also be derogatory (Helen is just a **clothes**horse)

clothes/close (see close/clothes)

coarse/course

coarse: A roughness in manner or appearance (he had a **coarse** manner that was unacceptable to his employers); a rough texture in material (the skirt had a **coarse** feeling that I didn't like); vulgar language (he told some very **coarse** jokes)

course: A field of study (the **course** I am taking will assist me to secure a good job); the location of some sporting events (we went to the golf **course** to have a friendly game); an expression (**of course** I will be going to see the procession); a term of duration (the wild weather has run its **course**)

coat/cote

coat: An outer covering (you really need a thick **coat** in cold weather; the house could do with another **coat** of paint); to gloss over (I will **coat** this refusal with some kind words)

cote: A stall or shed used as a shelter for birds or animals [e.g., dove **cote**, sheep **cote**] or to store items [e.g., **cote** for turnips]

colonel/kernel

colonel: A high-ranking officer in the armed forces (**Colonel** James was honored for his leadership in the Vietnam War)

kernel: The core that provides basic services for all other parts of a computer's operating system; a softer part inside the shell of a nut or stone fruit that is usually edible; also refers to the important part of a plan, subject, discussion (she addressed the **kernel** point in her introduction)

complement/compliment

complement: Refers to something that completes (they had a full **complement** to compete in the school sports; the bus had a full **complement** for the trip); also to suit (this scarf will be the perfect **complement** to your dress)

compliment: To praise (she blushed when she received the **compliment** that she was beautiful); sometimes used to insult (he gave her a backhanded **compliment**)

compliment/complement (see complement/compliment)

coo/coup

coo: The sound doves and pigeons make; the sound of a parent or adult when talking to a baby (John couldn't bear it when he heard his parents **coo** to the new baby)

coup: A takeover or usurping of power, often violent, in politics, business, the armed forces, etc. (it was an unexpected **coup** when the people regained power from the dictator) coral/choral (see choral/coral)

cord/cored/chord (see chord/cord/cored)

core/corps

> **core:** The center of a piece of fleshy fruit (David wanted his mother to take the **core** out of the apple before he ate it); the central or most important part (the **core** of his argument; they comprised the **core** of the government); in physics, the **core** of the reactor

> **corps:** An army group (the U.S. Army **Corps** of Engineers is highly respected worldwide); a specific group of people (Kevin was a member of the diplomatic **corps**)

cored/chord/cord (see chord/cord/cored)

corps/core (see core/corps)

correspondence/correspondents

> **correspondence:** Written communication to inform, elicit a response, or answer a query (answering all the **correspondence** you receive can be a chore); also relates to similarity (there is no **correspondence** between the rules governing the United States and those that control a dictatorship in a Third World country)

> **correspondents:** People who communicate by letters; news reporters who send stories and photos to newspapers and television stations (covering the war in Afghanistan can be a hazardous task for the **correspondents**)

correspondents/correspondence (see correspondence/
correspondents)

cote/coat (see coat/cote)

council/counsel

> **council:** A group of people elected to carry out certain
> duties [e.g., a city **council**, the World **Council** of
> Churches] (there are often heated debates at the weekly
> **council** meeting)

> **counsel:** Advice (Janet was desperate to seek **counsel**
> when her husband left her); or to give advice (the
> minister **counselled** her when her mother died)

counsel/council (see council/counsel)

coup/coo (see coo/coup)

course/coarse (see coarse/course)

coward/cowered

> **coward:** A faint-hearted person who lacks courage in a
> dangerous or difficult situation (David quickly realized
> that his friend was a **coward** by running away and
> leaving him to deal with the attackers)

> **cowered:** Past tense of "cower": to crouch in fear or
> shame with knees bent (she **cowered** in fear when her
> drunk husband accused her of having an affair)

cowered/coward (see coward/cowered)

creak/creek

creak: A noise made by an unoiled hinge when opening a door; movement of floorboards when the temperature changes, particularly at night (Sarah repeatedly nudged her husband in the night, fearing a burglar, when she heard a **creak**)

creek: A small stream, tributary, or narrow inlet from the coast (Ken loved to catch tadpoles in the **creek**); a slang term meaning you are in trouble (Alan remarked to his friend when his shares fell dramatically in price, "I'm up the **creek** without a paddle")

creek/creak (see creak/creek)

crewel/cruel

crewel: A fine yarn used for embroidery; a type of needle used for embroidering (she searched everywhere for her **crewel** needle to finish embroidering the flowers on the dress)

cruel: Causing pain and suffering (many consider it **cruel** to whip horses to win a race); a description of someone who takes satisfaction in inflicting pain (he was a **cruel** man who frequently hit his children)

crews/cruise

crews: Men and women who comprise various ships' companies (mutinies in the 18th century were a way **crews** could remove a sadistic or inept captain)

cruise: A trip on a passenger ship usually for pleasure (a popular **cruise** to take goes around the Greek Islands) cruel/crewel (see crewel/cruel)

cruise/crews (see crews/cruise)

cue/queue

cue: A long, thin rod used in billiards (he used his **cue** with great skill to sink the eight ball and win the game); a signal for a person to do something (the **cue** in the play for her to faint was the entrance of her father; the firing of a gun was the **cue** for the racers to run; the father pointing at the clock was a **cue** for the children to go to bed)

queue: A line of people (the **queue** for tickets extended to the next block)

currant/current

currant: A small, round berry often dried and used in fruit pies, biscuits, and curries (my favorite treat is a currant pie)

current: The present time; something that is happening now (I watch the **current** news on the television each night; my **current** electricity bill is much higher than the last one); water that is running in a river or stream (Kevin always tells the children not to swim in the river if the **current** is fast); electrical term referring to the flow of electricity (the **current** running through most power points is either 110 or 240 volts)

current/currant (see currant/current)

cygnet/signet

cygnet: A young swan

signet: A ring often with a small seal or engraving (Philip was proud of the **signet** ring with his initials engraved given to him by his father); an official seal authenticating a document (Henry VIII placed his **signet** on the paper to demolish the monasteries)

cymbal/symbol

cymbal: A percussion instrument consisting of two brass circular plates that are struck together (the noise of the **cymbal** can be very successful in waking up the audience at a symphony concert)

symbol: Something that stands for or suggests something else (the cross is a **symbol** of Christianity; in mathematics the **symbol** + means to add)

Czech/check (see check/Czech)

≳ D ≲

dam/damn

dam: A barrier to stop the flow of water usually across a river or stream (the world-famous Aswan High **Dam** is in Egypt); the female parent of a domestic animal (the horse's lineage shows the **dam** as Belle of the Ball and the sire, Black Knight)

damn: To censure or criticize (the critic would often **damn** plays after a first-night viewing); to curse (I **damn** you to hell); colloquial: a swear word damn/dam (see dam/damn)

days/daze

> **days:** Twenty-four-hour periods (there are seven **days** in a week); special events (Christmas and Boxing **days** are usually public holidays); referring to present times (these **days** it is difficult to make ends meet)
>
> **daze:** To be in shock or to stupefy (I was in a **daze** all day when I heard the news of the accident)

daze/days (see days/daze)

dear/deer

> **dear:** Describing a beloved person or close friend (my **dear** friend Eleanor is visiting me this week); a salutation used to begin a letter (**Dear** Sir or Madam); to indicate expense (it is a very **dear** vase); to express sympathy (Oh **dear** me, that is so awful)
>
> **deer:** A four-legged animal with horns or antlers (*Bambi* was an animated film about a **deer**); a particular type of deer (a famous **deer** is Rudolph the red-nosed rein**deer**)

deer/dear (see dear/deer)

dense/dents

> **dense:** To be crowded or compacted together (it was difficult to make your way through the **dense** forest; there was a **dense** crowd waiting at the airport to greet the returning Olympic Games competitors); to be

stupid or ignorant (you are so **dense**; I can't believe you forgot to pay your income tax)

dents: Hollows or impressions on an object as a result of blunt-edged blows or a collision (Vic noticed the number of **dents** on the side of his car as a result of the collision with a bicycle); colloquial: to have a lesser amount of money (buying the house and making renovations have certainly made a few **dents** in my savings)

dents/dense (see dense/dents)

descent/dissent

descent: A downward motion; descending (the hikers found the **descent** as difficult as the climb up the mountain; the **descent** down the stairway was quite hazardous); sinking to a lower level (everyone agreed that if he continued to drink heavily, he would make a quick **descent** into alcoholism)

dissent: Difference in opinion or sentiment; disagreement (there was much **dissent** in the community regarding the proposed development)

desert/dessert

desert: To abandon or leave a person or place with no intention of returning (her decision to **desert** her children was not taken lightly); to abscond from the military without intending to return (he made plans to **desert** the army when they suffered heavy casualties)

dessert: The last course of dinner, usually a sweet dish such as cake, pudding, ice cream, etc. (Johnny always ate less of the Sunday roast in anticipation of **dessert**)

dessert/desert (see desert/dessert)

dew/due

dew: Moisture that forms as droplets after condensation, particularly at night when the temperature falls (**dew**drops are visible on the flowers)

due: Expected time of arrival (the train is **due** at 6 p.m.); the required time of payment (your payment is **due** now; membership fees are **due** on January 1); owing to (**due** to exceptional circumstances, the show has been cancelled)

die/dye

die: To cease to live (she will **die** if she doesn't have an operation); to fail to exist (the truth will **die** with him); to fade away (the noise will **die** down when the machines are turned off); colloquial: to crave (I would **die** for a beer); irreversible decision (the **die** has been cast); the singular form of dice

dye: A color or tint (she uses **dye** in her hair to make it blonder)

disc/disk

disc: A thin, flat, round plate or similar (new model cars are fitted with **disc** brakes); anatomical: a disc in the spine (she had great pain when the **disc** in her back prolapsed)

disk: A storage unit for a computer (it is wise to back up your computer files on a **disk**)

discreet/discrete

discreet: Wise, cautious (Imogen overheard the conversation, and decided to be **discreet** and not repeat what was said); not flamboyant (her attire for the interview was very **discreet**—tailored and suitable)

discrete: Separate, distinct, not continuous (the school is separated into two **discrete** areas)

discrete/discreet (see discreet/discrete)

disk/disc (see disc/disk)

dissent/descent (see descent/dissent)

do/doe/dough

do: A musical note, first of the series in a scale [i.e., **do**, re, mi, fa, so, la, ti]

doe: A female deer or antelope; also a female kangaroo, goat, or rabbit

dough: Flour combined with other ingredients [e.g., yeast and water] to make bread (you must knead the **dough** until it is soft); colloquial: money (he makes a lot of **dough** from selling pies at the football game)

doe/dough/do (see do/doe/dough)

done/dun

done: Past participle of "do" (John had **done** his best to ensure his election campaign would be successful); completed (the list was **done**); ready, as in cooking (the roast seems to be almost **done**); colloquial: to be tired (after lifting the load of heavy bricks, Jack was completely **done in**)

dun: A dull color (painting the walls a **dun** color made the room gloomy)

dough/do/doe (see do/doe/dough)

douse/dowse

douse: To throw water over or plunge into water or similar (they decided to **douse** Eric with soft drink as a joke); colloquial: to put out or extinguish (please **douse** the candle before you go to bed)

dowse: To use a divining rod to search for underground water or minerals

dowse/douse (see douse/dowse)

draft/draught

draft: A preliminary sketch or plan (the council planner prepared a rough **draft** of the proposed new library); an outline or preliminary attempt of an essay, report, letter, or writing in general (the author threw the first **draft** of her novel into the wastebasket); conscription (he was fearful he would be included in the first army **draft** to fight in the war)

draught: A current of air (most people shiver when they feel a **draught** of air); beer drawn from a keg (I prefer **draught** beer over bottled)

draught/draft (see draft/draught)

drier/dryer

drier: A comparative adverb (today is much **drier** than yesterday, when it rained all day)

dryer: An appliance that dries clothes (many people are reluctant to use a clothes **dryer**, as they believe it uses too much energy)

dryer/drier (see drier/dryer)

ducked/duct

ducked: Past tense of "duck": to avoid or leave (he **ducked** when he saw the ball coming toward him; she **ducked** out to get the laundry off the line outside before it rained)

duct: Conduit, tube, or canal through which gas, air, water, or other substances are conveyed (the air **duct** in the office was blocked, causing many to complain); anatomically: a tube in the body for the passage of fluids, [e.g., tear **duct**]

duct/ducked (see ducked/duct)

due/dew (see dew/due)

dun/done (see done/dun)

dye/die (see die/dye)

≥ E ≤

earn/urn

earn: To gain by effort (I intend to **earn** my living by being the best plumber in the city); to deserve or merit (Helen hoped to **earn** a merit badge for her effort in raising funds for her school)

urn: A vase, often earthenware, usually with a pedestal (Jane admired the beautiful **urn** that was in the entrance hall); also used to contain the ashes of someone cremated (Anne buried the **urn** containing the ashes of her father under his favorite rosebush)

eave/eve

eave: Usually in plural form, a projecting edge of a roof

eve: The time immediately before an event (Christmas **Eve** is an exciting day for children; on the **eve** of her wedding, the bride was unable to sleep); also used poetically to refer to evening

eh/a/A (see a/A/eh)

eight/ate (see ate/eight)

ere/heir/air (see air/ere/heir)

eve/eave (see eave/eve)

ewe/yew/you

ewe: A female sheep

yew: A coniferous tree (many **yew** trees are found in churchyards)

you: A personal pronoun that is used in both singular and plural forms (are **you** and Jim buying that house?; how many of **you** are coming to the party?)

ewes/use/yews

ewes: A number of female sheep

use: To apply or utilize (Joan likes to **use** her best dinnerware when she has guests; I will **use** every opportunity I can to convince you of the benefits of having insurance)

yews: A number of yew trees

eye/I/aye (see aye/eye/I)

eyelet/islet

eyelet: A small, usually round, hole in cloth or leather through which lace, ribbon, or cord can be passed (Emily watched her mother thread pink ribbon through each **eyelet** in her new dress)

islet: A small island similar to cays found in the Bahamas or the West Atlantic

≷ F ≷

facts/fax

facts: Something that happened, a truth or reality (that World War I occurred between 1914 and 1918 is a known **fact**; historians and scientists both attempt to determine the **facts**); often used to bolster someone's opinion (the **facts** of these matters are hard to determine, however we are certain …)

fax: An abbreviation of "facsimile," meaning to copy; a method of transmission that involves scanning, transmitting, and receiving graphic and printed material via a telephone line (I hope you received my **fax** of the plans for the proposed building); also refers to the actual facsimile machine (my **fax** hasn't worked since I changed my telephone number)

faint/feint

faint: A feeling of weakness or a brief loss of consciousness (Shirley felt **faint** and asked if she could have a glass of water); lacking brightness or clarity (it was only a **faint** image and lacked detail); a possibility of success (I had a **faint** hope that I would be appointed the new director)

feint: A movement designed to deceive, particularly used in boxing (he learned how to **feint** with his left hand and strike a blow with his right)

fair/fare

fair: An event often to support a charity where there are stalls of goods on sale and possibly side shows (the annual church **fair**, with its home-baked cakes is always a favorite; children love trying to win a prize by knocking down the glass bottles at the **fair**); as an adjective, used to describe the weather, appearance, or an equitable decision (it is a **fair** day; she has a **fair** complexion as well as **fair** hair; it was a **fair** distribution of funds); an expression of length of time (I had to wait a **fair** amount of time to receive my inheritance)

fare: The amount of money charged for a journey by plane, train, bus, or taxi (Cecily was upset when she had to pay more for her train **fare** than she expected); also refers to food (the **fare** on the menu includes chicken, veal, and duck); also to a state of being (I **fare** pretty well on my pension)

fare/fair (see fair/fare)

fate/fête

fate: A mystical force that determines our life, destiny, or fortune (it was **fate** that he met his future wife while on vacation; it was **fate** that I stopped to buy the winning lottery ticket at that convenience store)

fête: A function usually to raise money for schools, churches, charities, similar to a bazaar or fair (our school **fête** was well attended by parents, teachers, and friends); to extol the virtues of a person, or to celebrate, mainly used in the past tense (he was **fêted** by the public for his charitable donations)

faun/fawn

faun: A mythological Roman god worshipped by shepherds and farmers, represented by a man with ears, and having the horns and tail of a goat, and supposedly very lusty (the slang word "horny" possibly arose from the association of lustiness with the **faun**)

fawn: A young deer (the **fawn** Bambi was immortalized by Disney in the film *Bambi*); to be servile to someone (I have never known anyone to **fawn** over his boss the way Jim does); a very light brown color (that **fawn** dress certainly didn't suit Jennifer's complexion)

faux/foe

faux: An imitation (Imogen was criticized by some of her friends for wearing a **faux** fur); also part of the phrase **faux pas**, meaning to make a false step, to slip up (Henry made a **faux pas** when he introduced the speaker with the wrong name)

foe: An enemy, opponent (the men quickly realized that the man approaching holding a gun was a **foe**, not a friend)

fawn/faun (see faun/fawn)

fax/facts (see facts/fax)

faze/phase

faze: To cause to feel uncertainty (he did not **faze** me when he interjected during my lecture)

phase: A stage of development (children pass from one **phase** to another as they grow and develop); an astronomical term referring to the appearance of a planet or the moon; a term used in biology and zoology

feat/feet

feat: An extraordinary act or accomplishment (climbing Mount Everest is an amazing **feat** of skill and endurance)

feet: The appendages at the end of legs (humans have two **feet** but dogs have four **feet**); a measurement of distance in the imperial system in contrast to metric (there are 24 inches in 2 **feet**); colloquial: to overwhelm (she was **swept off her feet** when he presented her with a huge diamond ring and asked her to marry him); to be self-sufficient (John, you have to **stand on your own two feet** if you want to succeed in business)

feet/feat (see feat/feet)

feint/faint (see faint/feint)

fête/fate (see fate/fête)

few/phew

few: A small number (only a **few** turned up to hear the candidate speak); infrequent (there were only a **few** sunny days this month)

phew: An exclamation (**Phew!** How close was that?)

file/phial

file: A collection of papers, photos, etc. located in a filing cabinet or on a computer (Kim was upset when she couldn't find the **file** her boss requested); an instrument used to cut through or smooth (she calmly trimmed her nails with her nail **file**); a number of people, animals, etc. in a line (the platoon followed the track in single **file**)

phial: A small container or bottle for liquids (the spy carried a **phial** of poison ready to use in an emergency)

find/fined

find: To locate or to discover something missing (I need to **find** the key to the car or I won't make my appointment on time)

fined: A financial punishment (Geoff was **fined** for speeding)

fined/find (see find/fined)

finish/Finnish

finish: To complete (Holly was pleased she was able to **finish** her test with minutes to spare); to use up (Stephen was keen to **finish** the remainder of the jam in the jar); a decisive end (they fought to the **finish**); a final coat of varnish, etc. (after a series of disasters, he finally had the **finish** on the table that he wanted); colloquial: the end (this last financial disaster was the **finish** of me)

Finnish: A person born in Finland

Finnish/finish (see finish/Finnish)

fir/fur

fir: The name of an evergreen coniferous tree (we always select a **fir** tree to decorate for Christmas)

fur: The hairy outer covering of animals (Airedale terrier dogs have brown and black curly **fur**); a pure or synthetic wool lining in slippers, boots, or shoes (Marion loved to wear her **fur**-lined boots when the weather was cold)

fishing/phishing

fishing: Casting a line into a river or sea to catch fish (Kevin took his boys **fishing** every weekend); colloquial: angling for a compliment or obtaining information (Susan was **fishing** for a compliment when she asked her boyfriend how he liked her new hairstyle)

phishing: Adjective describing fraudulent e-mails, letters, or phone calls that request or initiate a scam to get sensitive personal information (Gayle received a **phishing** call promising a holiday to Hawaii for only $100 if she paid by credit card immediately)

flair/flare

flair: An ability or talent (Marie had a **flair** for designing unusual clothes and eventually opened her own dress shop)

flare: A bright light usually short-lived (the distress **flare** was sighted by a passing ship); a sudden burst of temper (he was known to have a short fuse and **flare** up in a temper); an unexpected increase in illness (he had a **flare-up** of gout)

flare/flair (see flair/flare)

flea/flee

flea: A small wingless insect that bites humans and animals (our dogs are protected from **fleas** because we chemically treat them once a month)

flee: To run from (Heather had to **flee** the house when the earthquake shook the area)

flecks/flex

flecks: Tiny specks or spots (she hated to see **flecks** of paint everywhere after her husband's attempt at painting the house)

flex: To bend joints, parts of the body (he used to **flex** his muscles to try and impress girls); a small, flexible electrical cable or wire (most electricians carry at least one roll of **flex**)

flee/flea (see flea/flee)

flew/flu/flue

flew: Past tense of "to fly" (the birds **flew** away when they heard the gun)

flu: An abbreviation of the illness "influenza" (many of the office staff were absent because they had the **flu**)

flue: A duct or passageway for gases, smoke, etc. to escape (we need to clean out the **flue** in the chimney each year)

flex/flecks (see flecks/flex)

flocks/phlox

flocks: Groups of animals or birds (**flocks** of birds flew over as they migrated southward; **flocks** of sheep waited patiently to be shorn); also can refer to a crowd (**flocks** of people went to watch the final of the soccer game)

phlox: A perennial or annual plant that has clusters of reddish, purple, or white flowers found mainly in North America (some **phlox** flower in autumn, others in spring)

floe/flow

floe: A sheet of floating ice (passengers on the ship stared in amazement at the **floe** of ice floating in the Antarctic Ocean)

flow: Indicates movement (the conductor of an orchestra can make the music **flow**; the sewage will **flow** into the ocean unless they make immediate repairs)

flour/flower

flour: A finely ground meal of wheat or other grain mostly used in cooking (she was asked if she used self-raising or plain **flour** in her bread); a fine powder (**flour** and water can be used successfully as a paste)

flower: The decorative and colorful part of any plant (the red rose is regarded as the **flower** of love, so many men send a bunch to their sweetheart on Valentine's Day); used to indicate blooming (this plant should **flower** in the spring; she is in the **flower** of her youth) flow/floe (see floe/flow)

flower/flour (see flour/flower)

flu/flue/flew (see flew/flu/flue)

flue/flew/flu (see flew/flu/flue)

foaled/fold

foaled: Past tense of " to foal": to give birth to a foal (she **foaled** at night and everyone was excited to see the foal struggle to stand upright)

fold: To place one corner to another to reduce in size or to double over, particularly with paper, clothes, and large items such as blankets, sheets, tablecloths, and towels (it is important to **fold** clothes properly to eliminate creases); an enclosure for animals, particularly sheep (they herded the sheep into the **fold** to keep them safe)

foe/faux (see faux/foe)

fold/foaled (see foaled/fold)

for/fore/four

for: In favor of (he is **for** freedom of speech); as a purpose (Jack and Jill went **for** a walk up the hill; Henry gave a dinner **for** all the people who assisted in his campaign; Hilary was all **for** going out to dinner); used in connection with (we need to use a large vase **for** these flowers); a particular aptitude (she has an eye **for** modern art); colloquial: to admire (he has **an eye for** pretty girls)

fore: In front (he is at the **fore**front of everyone else; he has a very wrinkled **fore**head); the shout a golfer gives to warn those ahead of a golf ball coming (we all shudder when we hear "**fore**" shouted, particularly if we are the ones straight ahead)

four: A cardinal number as the symbol 4; depicts this number of items or persons (Mom, can we have **four** pieces of candy, please?)

forbear/forebear

forbear: To refrain from or to cease (he agreed to **forbear** swearing at his young children)

forebear: An ancestor (a convict from England was my **forebear**)

fore/four/for (see for/fore/four)

forebear/forbear (see forbear/forebear)

foreword/forward

foreword: An introduction or preface to a book, written by someone other than the author (the publishers were pleased when the former prime minister agreed to write the **foreword**)

forward: Moving toward something ahead (I moved **forward** toward the front of the line; I look **forward** to the time when I can retire); a sports position on soccer, basketball, hockey, etc. teams (he is regarded as the best **forward** on the team); a description of behavior (Jenny is a very **forward** person, pushing herself ahead of others more senior)

forth/fourth

forth: To go forward; hardly used today, regarded as archaic (he went **forth** into battle)

fourth: A number in a series (he is the **fourth** child)

forward/foreword (see foreword/forward)

foul/fowl

foul: Grossly smelly or offensive (there is a **foul** smell under the house; he uses extremely **foul** language); a sporting term to indicate a violation of the rules (the crowd shouted that there was a **"foul"** when the player fell to the ground after being tackled)

fowl: A bird, either singular or plural; can refer to wild birds but more often refers to domestic birds such as hens, geese, or ducks

four/for/fore (see for/fore/four)

fourth/forth (see forth/fourth)

fowl/foul (see foul/fowl)

franc/frank

franc: The monetary unit of countries where French is spoken, including France, Belgium, and Switzerland, before the introduction of the euro

frank: Open, honest, and candid (Henry was very **frank** when he told his boss the reason why he was not able to continue in the job); to mark a letter authorizing

delivery without having to place a stamp on the
envelope (it was Alan's job to **frank** the envelopes in
the office before posting them)

frank/franc (see franc/frank)

frays/phrase

frays: Noisy fights or brawls (the men were kicked out
of the pub after the public witnessed the **frays** among
a number of drinkers); to cause threads to come loose
from excess use (some of my clothes have **frays** at the
end of the sleeves from constant wear); colloquial: to
strain tempers (my temper constantly **frays** thin when
the children are home on break)

phrase: Two or more words arranged in a grammatical
sequence, acting as a unit; also refers to a number of
notes in music forming a recognizable pattern

frees/freeze/frieze

frees: To release or liberate (when Jennifer sees
mistreated birds in a cage, she **frees** them)

freeze: To harden water into ice (we needed to **freeze**
the water in trays to make ice cubes for the party); to
harden food by putting in the freezer (it is important
to **freeze** food you will be consuming later); colloquial:
to feel extreme cold (I will **freeze** if I go out in this
weather); to withhold payment (the bank is likely to
freeze your account if you are overdrawn); to stop
suddenly (the police told the bank robber to **freeze**)

frieze: A decorative design or band on wallpaper usually at the junction of the ceiling and wall (Sue was pleased when the **frieze** in her study was admired by her friends)

freeze/frieze/frees (see frees/freeze/frieze)

friar/fryer

friar: A brother or member of a Christian religious order such as the Franciscans and Carmelites (**Friar** Tuck is well known as one of Robin Hood's merry men)

fryer: A person who fries food or an appliance used for frying (we decided to use the electric **fryer** for the chips)

frieze/frees/freeze (see frees/freeze/frieze)

fryer/friar (see friar/fryer)

fur/fir (see fir/fur)

≥ G ≤

G/gee

G: Seventh letter of the English alphabet; a symbol in music (Rachmaninoff completed his "Prelude in **G** Minor" in 1901)

gee: An exclamation of surprise originating in America but also used in other countries (**gee**, is that really the time!?)

gaff/gaffe

gaff: A strong hook attached to a handle used to land large fish (Dennis was able to bring the tuna onto land using his **gaff**)

gaffe: A social mishap; a faux pas (she blushed when she realized she had made a **gaffe** when she introduced his secretary as his wife)

gaffe/gaff (see gaff/gaffe)

gage/gauge

gage: A challenge (he threw down his glove as a **gage** to provoke his rival to a duel); something deposited or given as security (a **gage** of $100,000 was deposited to ensure the show would proceed)

gauge: To estimate (I **gauge** the current temperature to be 26 degrees); a standard of measurement (my shotgun is 12 **gauge**); the distance between rails on which trains run (for a long time the railway **gauge** differed across the various states in Australia until the standard **gauge** of 4 feet, 8½ inches was introduced nationwide); an instrument that measures pressure, volume, etc.

gait/gate

gait: The way one walks (Eric has a very peculiar **gait** as a result of having one leg shorter than the other); the manner in which a horse moves (the horse's **gait** can vary from a trot, to a canter, to a gallop)

gate: An entrance to a garden, field, etc., constructed usually of wood or metal (it was a very ornamental **gate** that opened into the rose gardens on display)

gall/Gaul

gall: To be irritating, annoying, or impudent (he had such **gall** to boo out loud at the performance); bile, bitterness, associated with the gall bladder (some say you need your **gall bladder** removed)

Gaul: An ancient region in Western Europe roughly equivalent to modern France, Belgium, Luxembourg, and Germany west of the Rhine (Julius Caesar's campaigns against **Gaul**, known as the Gallic Wars, were fought in 58–51 BC)

gallop/Gallup/galop

gallop: The fastest gait of a horse (the horse began to **gallop** when it saw it was near home)

Gallup: A poll in which various voters representing a cross-section of the population are asked their intentions to assess the voting trends of the population (the **Gallup** poll indicated that it could be a hung parliament)

galop: A lively dance in three/four time popular in the 19th century

Gallup/galop/gallop (see gallop/Gallup/galop)

galop/gallop/Gallup (see gallop/Gallup/galop)

gamble/gambol

gamble: To take a chance (he took a **gamble** on the weather being fine and booked the tennis court; Judy took a **gamble** on the horse coming first in the derby and bet $1,000)

gambol: To leap about playfully; to frolic (the children liked to **gambol** in the garden)

gambol/gamble (see gamble/gambol)

gate/gait (see gait/gate)

gauge/gage (see gage/gauge)

Gaul/gall (see gall/Gaul)

gee/G (see G/gee)

genes/jeans

genes: Units of inheritance, a part of our DNA, that give us our individual traits such as hair color, eye color, blood type, etc. (Jane's blue eyes came from her mother's **genes**); a talent inherited from our parents (Simon's tenor voice is in his **genes**)

jeans: A rugged twilled cotton trouser, usually blue in color (**jeans** were first patented by Levi Strauss and Jacob Davis in 1873 in America)

gild/gilled/guild

gild: To cover with a thin layer of gold or gold paint, usually done to make the article more impressive; also used in the expression **gild the lily**, meaning the unnecessary use of adornment or to over-embellish (the expression **gild the lily** originated from Shakespeare's play *King John*)

gilled: To have gills, the respiratory organs of aquatic animals that breathe water to attain oxygen (the six-**gilled** shark is a large primitive shark that lives deep in the sea)

guild: In the Middle Ages, a group of people engaged in a particular trade or occupation, a precursor of the trade union, later represented merchants and owners of businesses (**guild** halls still exist in the 21st century, as do some **guilds**, such as the Pharmacy Guild of Australia)

gilled/guild/gild (see gild/gilled/guild)

gilt/guilt

gilt: A description of an object covered with a thin layer of gold, gold paint, or gold leaf (the **gilt** frame enhanced the portrait)

guilt: The act of feeling the blame for an action (he was full of **guilt** when he realized that his actions had caused his mother grief; the murderer confessed his **guilt** when he was apprehended)

glair/glare

glair: A preparation made from the white of an egg

glare: A strong, bright, dazzling light (the **glare** of the oncoming car's headlights caused Sarah to swerve to avoid a head-on collision); a fierce or long look (Henry's **glare** indicated that he was extremely unhappy with Alison's reply)

glare/glair (see glair/glare)

gnu/knew/new

gnu: A wildebeest, a South African animal similar to an ox (many tourists visiting South Africa hope to see a **gnu**)

knew: Past tense of "to know" (I **knew** him when he was a little boy; it was common knowledge that he **knew** more about the accident than he was telling anyone)

new: Describing something that has just been brought into being, or of recent origin or manufacture (Sylvia waxed lyrical over the charms of her **new** baby; this **new** drug on the market will assist you with your arthritis); recently arrived (he is **new** to the city, having just moved from Texas); the introduction of radical or different ideas (Simon's **new** system of accounting has resulted in greater efficiency)

gofer/gopher

gofer: A colloquial expression referring to a person, lowly in status, who runs errands (he is a **gofer** for all the bosses)

gopher: Any burrowing animal, but particularly the ground squirrels of western North America

gopher/gofer (see gofer/gopher)

gored/gourd

gored: The piercing of an animal or a human with a dagger, tusk, or horn (she hated going to bullfights, as she felt sick when a bull was **gored** by a matador or vice versa)

gourd: The fruit of a large climbing plant related to the squash and cucumber (the **gourd** is known as the "bitter melon" in England)

gorilla/guerrilla

gorilla: A large vegetarian ape found in western equatorial Africa (the **gorilla** has appeared in many movies, among them *King Kong* and *George of the Jungle*); colloquial: to describe someone big, ugly, and possibly brutal (keep away from him, for he is a **gorilla**)

guerrilla: One of a small band of independent soldiers or freedom fighters who harass enemy forces by sabotaging railways and destroying communications, etc.

gourd/gored (see gored/gourd)

grate/great

grate: A frame of metal bars used to contain ashes in a fireplace or to cover an opening (Susan's job was to clean the **grate** after last night's fire); to make one shudder or put on edge (her voice would **grate** on her students and they would squirm)

great: Important or significant (it was a **great** moment when the announcement was made that the war had ended); also relates to size (he is a **great** big, lazy slob)

grays/graze

grays: Various tints of the color between black and white; describing a number of gray horses (the announcer commented that it was mostly a field of **grays** in the race)

graze: To feed on grass or pastures, particularly sheep or cattle (the farmer had plenty of grass for his sheep to **graze** on except when there was a drought); to scrape the skin or touch something lightly (his mother told him he was likely to **graze** an arm or leg if he continued climbing the tree)

graze/grays (see grays/graze)

grease/Greece

grease: The oil or fat used in cooking; a lubricant (Rhys put some **grease** on his bicycle chain to make it run smoothly)

Greece: An ancient European country (the Olympics are believed to have originated in **Greece** in 776 BC)

great/grate (see grate/great)

Greece/grease (see grease/Greece)

grill/grille

grill: To cook under a flame as opposed to frying in a pan (Peter prefers to **grill** his steak because he is concerned about his diet); colloquial: to interrogate someone, particularly a person in custody (it is common practice for the police to **grill** people suspected of being involved in a murder)

grille: A metal or lattice shield often used to protect windows (after she was burglarized she had a **grille** installed over every window as protection); an ornamental, usually chrome, protective shield for the front of a car above the bumper bar (**grilles** on cars were very popular in the 1960s)

grille/grill (see grill/grille)

grisly/grizzly

grisly: Description of something gruesome that causes horror (it was a **grisly** murder)

grizzly: To complain or be irritable (Tom was **grizzly** all day because he did not sleep well the night before); a ferocious bear found in North America (they were warned not to enter the area because of the likelihood of **grizzly** bears being there)

grizzly/grisly (see grisly/grizzly)

groan/grown

groan: To make a deep sound of pain or grief (the mother made a mournful **groan** when told of the death of her son in an accident)

grown: Increase in size or height (our jacaranda tree has **grown** so quickly since we planted it)

grown/groan (see groan/grown)

guerrilla/gorilla (see gorilla/guerrilla)

guessed/guest

guessed: Making a random assessment (he **guessed** she was about 24 years old)

guest: A person who is invited to a home or event, or who is staying at a hotel (Fay was a welcome **guest** at our 25th anniversary dinner)

guest/guessed (see guessed/guest)

guild/gild/gilled (see gild/gilled/guild)

guilt/gilt (see gilt/guilt)

guise/guys

guise: An external or assumed appearance (he came in the **guise** of a friend)

guys: Colloquial: term for a number of men that now has been extended to include females ("Hi **guys**" is a popular inclusive greeting for both sexes when they meet); in Britain the name of the effigies of Guy Fawkes (the **guys** are burnt on a bonfire to celebrate Guy Fawkes' Night on November 5)

guys/guise (see guise/guys)

ꝫ H ꝭ

hail/hale

hail: To greet or to acknowledge (we will **hail** him as the defender of the people); also to attract attention (it is always difficult to **hail** a taxi after 11 p.m.); frozen ice (there was **hail** the size of golf balls on the lawn)

hale: To be healthy and full of vigor ("**hale and hearty**" is a very common expression to describe anyone in the best of health)

hair/hare

hair: The natural covering on a human's body and head as well as other mammals (his **hair**brush is so full of hairs, it won't be long before he needs a wig; I hate having dog **hair** on my couch); used to indicate a very small distance; colloquial: to annoy (Amy was always getting into someone's **hair**); to be frightened (her **hair** stood on end); to drink to become robust (to put **hair** on his chest); to show no emotion (she heard the jury's judgment without turning a **hair**)

hare: A rodent-type animal with long ears, similar to a rabbit but not as sociable (a **hare** less than one year old is called a leveret)

hale/hail (see hail/hale)

hall/haul

hall: The entrance to a building, also a wide corridor (Helen's house was much admired for its wide **hall** leading to the great room); also refers to a large building, meeting place, or assembly (the guild **hall** traditionally was used for meetings; accommodation for students (university **halls** provide rooms for country or overseas students)

haul: To pull or drag (it was Jim's job to **haul** away the trees after they had been cut down); to last the distance (they were all in for **the long haul**)

handle/Handel

handle: What everyone hangs on to when opening a door or cupboard (Jane has a very ornate **handle** on her front door); to manage (please **handle** this parcel with care); colloquial: to understand how to use something (he needs to **get a handle** on how to operate this machine or he will lose his job); colloquial: a person's name (his **handle** is Stephen)

Handel: Famous composer, George Frideric Handel was born in 1685 (**Handel** wrote the "Messiah," which is played every year at Christmas)

Handel/handle (see handle/Handel)

hangar/hanger

hangar: A large covered area for aircraft (small airfields have at least one **hangar** for planes to be kept while not in flight)

hanger: A useful object for hanging clothes (a **hanger** for men's trousers is usually provided in hotels and motels)

hanger/hangar (see hangar/hanger)

hare/hair (see hair/hare)

hart/heart

hart: A male deer over five years of age, particularly red deer

heart: The organ in all animals that keeps the blood circulating throughout the body (the **heart** is normally located on the left side of the chest); regarded also as the site of emotions (his **heart** ached when his sweetheart left him); used in many expressions: to be frank (I will have a **heart-to-heart** talk with him about his job prospects); to desire (I have **set my heart** on becoming the best surfer in the world)

haul/hall (see hall/haul)

hay/hey

hay: Grass that is cut and dried as fodder for animals (when there is a drought, it is difficult to obtain sufficient **hay** to feed all the animals); colloquial: to take advantage of every available opportunity (to **make hay** while the sun's shining); also colloquial: to go to bed (to **hit the hay**)

hey: A call or shout to attract attention ("**hey**, Richard")

heal/heel/he'll

heal: To make healthy (if you take this medicine, it will **heal** you); to free from distress (it takes a long time for the heart to **heal** after the death of a spouse or child)

heel: The back part of the foot behind and below the ankle (I hurt my **heel** when I was running); the part of the sock, stocking, or shoe that covers the bottom part of the foot (the **heel** of my shoe broke and I had to walk barefooted); used figuratively to indicate a weakness (gambling is his **Achilles' heel**); colloquial: a despicable or dishonest person (he is such a **heel** that he stole money from his mother's purse to pay his gambling debts); a command for dog obedience (his master told the dog to **heel**)

he'll: A contraction of "he will" (**he'll** be home later)

hear/here

hear: To be able to perceive sound through your auditory senses (Jean was thrilled to **hear** the roar of the sea and the waves pounding on the beach after many years living in the countryside)

here: At this place (we are so pleased to see you **here** at church); used for emphasis (**here** today we can see the results of neglect on the electorate); a common expression referring to life and death, acceptance (**here today and gone tomorrow**)

heard/herd

heard: Past tense of the verb "to hear" (I **heard** the trains shunting through the night; she nodded her head to indicate she had **heard** him)

herd: A number of animals, especially cattle or sheep (it is annoying sometimes when you are driving to wait for the **herd** of sheep to wander across the road); also to drive the animals (it is a sign of the times when stockmen use bikes instead of horses to **herd** the cattle); used derogatively when describing a number of people (the **herd** is gathering again!)

heart/hart (see hart/heart)

he'd/heed

he'd: A contraction of "he had" or "he would" (**he'd** used all his money to buy that car; **he'd** need to do better than that if he wants to be selected for the team)

heed: To listen to or take the advice of someone; to observe (I **heed** what you are saying but I don't think I will take any action at the present time)

heed/he'd (see he'd/heed)

heel/he'll/heal (see heal/heel/he'll)

heir/air/ere (see air/ere/heir)

he'll/heal/heel (see heal/heel/he'll)

herd/heard (see heard/herd)

here/hear (see hear/here)

heroin/heroine

heroin: A drug derived from morphine originally used as a sedative but now regarded as a dangerous substance (the number of deaths from **heroin** use has reached staggering figures over the years)

heroine: The principal female in a play or book; a female hero (the term "**heroine**" is rarely used today as it is regarded as a sexist description)

heroine/heroin (see heroin/heroine)

hertz/hurts

hertz: A unit of frequency (Hz) defined as one cycle per second, which is used to measure sound, light, and radio waves (the average human ear can detect sound waves between 20 and 20,000 **Hz**); a large rental car hire firm in Europe, United States, and Australia (**Hertz** was one of the first firms to offer rental electric cars)

hurts: To cause pain (Philip always **hurts** Jonathan when he twists his arm as a joke); to be in physical or emotional pain (it **hurts** every time I try to ride a bicycle; Jennifer **hurts** when she remembers the death of her husband); to suffer economic stress (the community **hurts** in an economic downturn)

hew/hue/Hugh

hew: To chop down or strike forcibly with an axe, sword, or similar tool (he was told to **hew** a path through the tangled mess at the bottom of the garden); to persist or continue to do something and not change (against all opposition, James will continue to **hew** to his plan to ensure equal pay for males and females)

hue: A variety of color (red is a **hue**, as are blue, green, and purple)

Hugh: A man's name

hey/hay (see hay/hey)

hi/high

hi: A greeting or acknowledgment ("**hi, Mom**")

high: Tall or lofty (this building is so **high**, I am frightened even to look out of the window); to describe rank (he is **high** up in the foreign office); to be elated (she is **on a high**); the effect of drugs (you can't reason with him, he is **as high as a kite**); to take a risk (to play for **high** stakes)

hide/hied

hide: To put something somewhere so no one can locate it (I will **hide** the presents in the wardrobe so Hollie can't find them); to conceal (David decided to **hide** his feelings from his girlfriend); the skin of an animal (the rhinoceros has a very tough **hide**); colloquial: to describe someone insensitive (he has a **hide** like an elephant)

hied: Past tense of "to hie": to run off quickly (he **hied** off when he knew it was his turn to pay for the round of drinks)

hied/hide (see hide/hied)

high/hi (see hi/high)

higher/hire

higher: Used to indicate that something is taller than something else (the Burj Khalifa in Dubai is **higher** than the Empire State Building in New York); figuratively: to indicate superiority (he has a **higher** position in the government than his brother)

hire: To engage for payment (I intend to **hire** a car to drive to the airport)

him/hymn

him: A personal pronoun (I knew it was **him** the moment I saw his photograph)

hymn: A song in praise of God; also a national anthem ("God Save our Gracious Queen" is the national **hymn** of Great Britain); can be an anthem of the military, naval, or air forces (the United States Marines' **Hymn** begins with the line "From the Halls of Montezuma, to the shores of Tripoli")

hire/higher (see higher/hire)

ho/hoe

ho: An exclamation used to attract attention ("**tally ho**" is the usual rallying cry for a hunt)

hoe: A tool with a long handle used to break up and loosen earth to make it suitable for cultivation

hoard/horde

hoard: To store away for preservation or later use (Jim would **hoard** so much in the garage, he was never able to find anything)

horde: A great number of animals or humans (we had to run fast to avoid the **horde** of elephants coming straight toward us)

hoarse/horse

hoarse: Refers mainly to a human whose voice has become slightly rough and deep (when she asked the doctor what was causing her to be **hoarse**, he said it was an infection in the vocal cords)

horse: A large, solid-hoofed quadruped animal, usually domesticated, used for riding, racing, or pulling drays on farms (Phar Lap was foaled in New Zealand and later became Australia's most famous race**horse**); colloquial: to act foolishly (she would always **horse around** to attract attention); a slang term for heroin hoe/ho (see ho/hoe)

hoes/hose

> **hoes:** A number of long-handled implements used for breaking up and loosening earth for cultivation; also refers to the action of preparing the land for cultivation (he works from dawn to dusk when he **hoes** the land to prepare for the next crop)

> **hose:** A long, flexible rubber tube used for watering the garden or hosing down the house or car (the dog loves to chase the **hose** when I am watering the lawn); colloquial: referring to stockings, socks, and pantyhose

hold/holed

> **hold:** To grasp (I will **hold** onto you until the police come); to dominate or control (he has a **hold** over her and she does whatever he wants); to retain (I will **hold on** to this job even if it means working longer hours); colloquial: to regain self-control (please get a **hold** over yourself, as everyone is looking at you); in abeyance (I will put the matter **on hold** until I hear from you)

> **holed:** A garment or similar that has a large number of holes (these stockings are so **holed** I can't wear them)

hole/whole

> **hole:** An opening or excavation (the recent floods have left a large pot**hole** in the road); the small openings in the ground on a golf course (this is an 18-**hole** golf course); colloquial: to hide oneself from embarrassment (I could have dug a **hole** after I made that stupid comment); colloquial: to be in trouble (I

am **in a hole** over the comments I made on television); colloquial: a sub-standard house or area (this is a **hole** of a place to live in)

whole: Entire, complete (you must eat the **whole** dinner and not just the sweets!)

holed/hold (see hold/holed)

holey/holy/wholly

holey: To be full of holes (moths must have eaten this blanket, as it is so **holey**)

holy: Sacred or divine (she is a **holy** person, devoted to the service of man and God)

wholly: Entirely or completely (he is **wholly** rapt watching television)

holy/wholly/holey (see holey/holy/wholly)

horde/hoard (see hoard/horde)

horse/hoarse (see hoarse/horse)

hose/hoes (see hoes/hose)

hour/our

hour: An amount of time comprising 60 minutes or 1/24th of a day (I have waited exactly one **hour** for you to arrive!); colloquial: to mean an approximate time (it will take only an **hour** of your time for me to demonstrate this fully to you)

our: Belonging to us (it is **our** home, not yours)

hue/Hugh/hew (see hew/hue/Hugh)

Hugh/hew/hue (see hew/hue/Hugh)

humerus/humorous

humerus: The long bone that extends from the shoulder to the elbow in humans and similarly in animals (the elbow, the end of the **humerus**, is often called the "funny bone" because of the association with the word "humorous")

humorous: Funny, amusing, being able to make people laugh (some people are naturally **humorous**)

humorous/humerus (see humerus/humorous)

hurts/hertz (see hertz/hurts)

hymn/him (see him/hymn)

≳ I ≲

I/aye/eye (see aye/eye/I)

idle/idol

idle: Not working, unemployed, or being lazy (the bike is lying **idle** because nobody has fixed the puncture; he is just an **idle**, good-for-nothing man)

idol: A worshipped image or person (many people worship an **idol** believing they will be rewarded; a pop or film star can be elevated to **idol** status); a person who is adored (she is my **idol**)

idol/idle (see idle/idol)

I'll/isle/aisle (see aisle/I'll/isle)

in/inn

in: A preposition (I will be **in** the office all day; he is **in** love; colloquial: to be part of the group (he is well **in** with all politicians); colloquial: to be in trouble (he is up to his neck **in** it); colloquial: the current fashion (black is the **in** color this winter)

inn: A hotel or tavern (The Junction **Inn** is one of our favorite places to have a meal and a drink)

incidence/incidents

incidence: The occurrence, rate, or likelihood of something happening (the **incidence** of children drowning in backyard pools has increased alarmingly over the past decade)

incidents: Events or occurrences (there have been two **incidents** in the region where young women have been attacked and robbed)

incidents/incidence (see incidence/incidents)

independence/independents

independence: Being free of control from others (Sarah reveled in her **independence** when she left home to share an apartment with her friends)

Independents: Mainly refers to members of political parties or intending candidates who are non-aligned with any political party (Many Americans say they're tired of the two-party system and would like more **Independents** to run for office)

independents/independence (see independence/ independents)

inn/in (see in/inn)

innocence/innocents

innocence: Pure, untainted, free from sin (the **innocence** of children is beautiful to see); also refers to being not guilty of a crime, accident, or incident (the man accused of stealing pleaded his **innocence** before the judge; the young boy declared his **innocence** when accused of hitting his brother)

innocents: Those who are free from guilt or sin (the young children are the **innocents** in this tussle between the mother and the father)

innocents/innocence (see innocence/innocents)

intense/intents

intense: Happening at a higher degree (the heat of the fire was so **intense** that they had to flee quickly; she was so **intense** when she was promoting her argument from the platform that she antagonized the moderate crowd)

intents: Something that is intended (the **intents** of the crowd were to see justice done); used often in the expression "**for all intents and purposes**" intents/intense (see intense/intents)

isle/aisle/I'll (see aisle/I'll/isle)

islet/eyelet (see eyelet/islet)

its/it's

its: A possessive pronoun, meaning belonging to (my cat is beautiful, with **its** thick and black coat; the house is very dreary and **its** dark windows only make it worse)

it's: A contraction of "it is" or "it has" (**it's** been a long time since we took a vacation)

it's/its (see its/it's)

≳ J ≲

jam/jamb

jam: A sticky substance of sugar and fruit used to spread on sandwiches (as a young child, she loved to smear **jam** not only on the bread but over the table, the wall, and everywhere she could reach); to cause people, cars, etc. to be packed tightly together (a traffic **jam** at rush hour is inevitable; I will try to **jam** all my clothes into one overnight bag); to play music together for pleasure (musicians **jam** together every Tuesday night at the local bar)

jamb: The vertical piece or surface forming the side of an opening in a door, window, or similar

jamb/jam (see jam/jamb)

jeans/genes (see genes/jeans)

jewel/joule

    jewel: A precious stone or gem often worn for personal adornment in a brooch, necklace, etc. (for their 40th wedding anniversary, her husband bought her a ring featuring a ruby **jewel**); colloquial: an appreciated person (Bert, you are a **jewel!**)

    joule: A unit of work or energy; also a measure of the energy content of food (in metric form a kilojoule equals 1,000 **joules**)

joule/jewel (see jewel/joule)

⋛ K ⋚

kernel/colonel (see colonel/kernel)

key/quay/cay (see cay/key/quay)

knave/nave

    knave: An unprincipled rogue or dishonest man (after being engaged for six years, the **knave** left her at the altar); also the jack in a deck of playing cards (there are four **knaves** in a deck of cards: hearts, diamonds, clubs, and spades)

    nave: The hub of a wheel; the main part of a Christian church, extending from the entrance to the area around the altar

knead/kneed/need

knead: To press, fold, and stretch dough, clay, etc. to make pastry or bread, or mold into pottery (there is a certain feeling of elation when you **knead** clay to finally produce a piece of pottery); also a term used in massaging (the masseur will **knead** your back to remove tension)

kneed: To strike or hit someone with your knee (he **kneed** his attacker in the groin to stop him)

need: To want or require something (if Jennifer agrees to take in her sister's children, she will **need** a larger house)

kneed/need/knead (see knead/kneed/need)

knew/new/gnu (see gnu/knew/new)

knight/night

knight: In the middle ages, a mounted man serving a feudal lord, later a man of noble birth and military rank who followed the code of chivalry (Sir Lancelot was a **knight** of King Arthur's round table); a chess piece (the **knight** is shaped like a horse's head to distinguish it from other pieces); colloquial: to describe a man who is protective and supportive (he is her **knight in shining armor**)

night: The period of darkness between sunset and sunrise (she always looked forward to **night** after the children went to bed and the house was quiet and peaceful)

knit/nit

knit: To create a garment by looping and crossing wool using long needles or on a machine (Heather always offers to **knit** scarves for other family members); to create a bond between people (the community will **knit** together to fight the sale of heritage land)

nit: The egg or louse of a parasitic insect (the teacher hates to see a **nit** in the hair of a child because it usually means that other students also will be affected)

knob/nob

knob: A rounded object used to open a door, drawer, etc. (Kim pulled the **knob** on the kitchen cupboard so hard, it came off in her hand); a round head on a walking stick (he used the **knob** of his walking stick to fend off an attacker); a rounded mountain or hill (as children they often climbed the **knob**)

nob: Colloquial: the head (watch your **nob** as you go through that doorway)

knot/not

knot: The interlacing of two pieces of string, rope, cotton, etc. drawn tightly together (she needs to **knot** the ends of her pajama cords or her pants will fall down; the reef **knot** is a common **knot**)

not: A word, usually an adverb, used to express refusal, prohibition, negation, denial (I will **not** eat my vegetables; Monday is **not** a public holiday; it was **not** me; I did **not** do it)

know/no

know: To have knowledge about someone or something (did you **know** we have been married for 15 years in November?); to be acquainted with another person (I **know** you, as we met at Ron and Barbara's party last year); colloquial: to have information not available to others (he is **in the know** about who is likely to win the award)

no: To refuse; the opposite of yes (**no**, you are not going out tonight)

knows/noes/nose

knows: The knowledge someone else has about you or others or something (he **knows** I am likely to make a mistake when adding up figures)

noes: The plural of "no," used when counting those voting against a motion in a meeting (there are 15 votes for and 17 against, so the **noes** have it)

nose: The organ of smell and breathing on the front of the face in both humans and animals (Pinocchio's **nose** grew larger each time he told a lie); also refers to the front end of an aircraft; colloquially used in many expressions [e.g., to denote a good journalist able to ferret out information (he has a good **nose** for news); describing the actions of someone interfering or prying (she should keep her **nose** out of other people's business); referring to something that has a bad smell (that food is **on the nose**); or indicating someone who works hard (he has his **nose to the grindstone**); or someone being superior (she **looks down her nose** at everyone)]

≥ L ≤

lacks/lax

lacks: To be deficient in something desirable, necessary, or customary (this argument **lacks** substance)

lax: To be negligent or careless (he is **lax** about turning the lights off when he goes out)

lade/laid

lade: To take on cargo; to dip or ladle (the lunch lady **lade** the chili into bowls)

laid: The past tense and participle of the verb "to lay" meaning to put down (she was **laid** to rest next to her husband in the cemetery)

laid/lade (see lade/laid)

lain/lane

lain: The past participle of the verb "to lie" (I had **lain** down to sleep)

lane: A narrow passageway through tracks, houses, or hedges (the boys often play in the **lane** behind the house); a narrow area between old tenement houses; a designated area on roads for buses, cars, or bicycles (drivers of cars will be fined if they travel in the bus **lane**)

lam/lamb

lam: A slang term meaning to run away (he is **on the lam** from the police)

lamb: A young sheep (children love to pet a **lamb** at the farm show); meat from a young sheep (a baked **lamb** dinner is a family favorite); colloquial: someone inexperienced and naïve (she was led like a **lamb** to the slaughter)

lama/llama

lama: A Tibetan or Mongolian Buddhist monk (the Tibetan Dalai **Lama** visited the people of Queensland, Australia, after the disastrous floods in 2011)

llama: A South American animal related to the camel with woolly hair and no hump (**llama** wool can be knitted into soft sweaters)

lamb/lam (see lam/lamb)

lane/lain (see lain/lane)

laps/lapse

laps: The plural term for the area of the part of the body from the waist to the knees when sitting (I pity the poor baby, who has been passed around all day and has sat on so many **laps**); circuits on a racing track or the distance swum in a pool (the racing car driver is now two **laps** in front of his next rival); to consume liquid with the tongue (our cat **laps** her milk without making a mess)

lapse: A slight error or misjudgment (it was a **lapse** on my part when I mentioned the party to which they hadn't been invited); to decline or become invalid (the hurt will **lapse** over time); a passing of time (after a **lapse** of two hours, the meter will expire); sinking to a lower level (the **lapse** into drunkenness wasn't noticeable for some time)

lapse/laps (see laps/lapse)

lax/lacks (see lacks/lax)

lay/lei

lay: To place or position something or someone (to **lay** down a baby in a crib; to **lay** down the law about what time to be home); referring to non-ordained persons who play a role in the church (Fiona is a **lay** preacher and often conducts the service at our church); the contours of the land (Richard knows the **lay** of the land)

lei: A garland of flowers, commonly seen in the Hawaiian Islands (when Rhys arrived in Honolulu he was greeted and a **lei** was placed around his neck)

lays/laze/leis

lays: Third person singular of "to lay" (he **lays** the photos out to make a selection)

laze: To be idle, relaxing, enjoying doing nothing (I love to **laze** about on the weekend and read the paper in bed)

leis: Plural of "lei" (the **leis** the girls put around our necks were made of beautiful red and white flowers)

laze/leis/lays (see lays/laze/leis)

lea/lee

lea: A meadow or grassland for pasturing animals

lee: The sheltered side away from the wind (go to the **lee** side and we will be protected from the wind)

leach/leech

leach: The slow removal of a mineral or chemical from soil or similar by the percolating of water, particularly rainwater (the farmers hope that the current heavy rain will **leach** any pesticides or industrial waste from the land)

leech: A blood-sucking worm (it was not uncommon for children to come out from swimming in a river with a **leech** on their leg); colloquial: a slang expression for attempting to gain the affections of someone for personal gain (she will **leech** on to him if she has a chance!)

lead/led

lead: A soft, malleable bluish-gray metal used for various purposes such as piping, soldering, plumbing, and in pencils (pencils contain either black **lead** or graphite); colloquial: to drive fast (he drives with a **lead** foot)

led: Past tense or participle of the verb "to lead" (he **led** the parade)

leak/leek

leak: A hole, usually small, that allows gas, water, or other substances to escape (we need to call a plumber to fix that **leak** in the bathroom); also, passing on information to people who were not the intended recipients (the organization found out who was responsible for the **leak** of the secret plans)

leek: A plant that is related to the onion but has a long cylindrical bulb, used in cooking (potato-**leek** soup is one of my favorites)

lean/lien

lean: The opposite of plump, meaning more muscle and less fat (I prefer a **lean** piece of steak); refers also to a lack of business or activity (it was a **lean** time for businesses in the recession); as a verb, refers to something or someone on a slant or not perpendicular (sit upright and don't **lean** on me!)

lien: A legal term meaning someone has a hold over a property until the debt is repaid (he was advised by his lawyer that his business partner had secured a **lien** over the business premises until he paid half the building costs incurred)

leased/least

leased: The rental of a house, building, car, etc. (I **leased** a car instead of buying one)

least: The minimum time or effort used to complete a task (it was the **least** I could do for you in the circumstances) least/leased (see leased/least)

led/lead (see lead/led)

lee/lea (see lea/lee)

leech/leach (see leach/leech)

leek/leak (see leak/leek)

lei/lay (see lay/lei)

leis/lays/laze (see lays/laze/leis)

lessen/lesson

> **lessen:** To abate or decrease; to be less (the announcer on the radio said the winds would **lessen** in the afternoon)

> **lesson:** An instructional period of time in school, college, etc. (I had a two-hour **lesson** at the driving school); something learned from an experience (it was a **lesson** to me not to drive through a red light); a reproof (this will teach you a **lesson** not to hit your baby sister!); a scripture reading (the **lesson** for today is from Mark 1)

lesson/lessen (see lessen/lesson)

levee/levy

> **levee:** An embankment occurring naturally from a buildup of silt from flooding or constructed by people to stop a river from overflowing (the **levee** built with sandbags was unsuccessful in stopping the floodwaters)

levy: To impose or collect a tax, fees, etc. (the government has put a **levy** on the import of luxury cars); to draft into military service (the **levy** to increase the number of troops to serve overseas was opposed by the public)

levy/levee (see levee/levy)

liar/lyre

liar: A person who tells untruths; a person who lies (he is such a **liar** that no one now believes anything he says)

lyre: Of Greek origin, a stringed instrument of the harp family having two curved arms connected at the upper end by a crossbar, commonly used to accompany a singer or a person reciting poetry

lie/lye

lie: A false statement with the intent to deceive; an untruth (she told him a **lie** that the coat was a bargain); a statement that is not actually true so as not to hurt (Jack told her a **white lie** that he liked her new hairstyle even though he thought it didn't suit her); to recline or to be in a prostate position (I need to **lie** down to get rid of this headache); to accept defeat (in the ring he tended to **lie down** and take the punishment)

lye: A strong alkaline solution particularly used in washing; a detergent

lien/lean (see lean/lien)

light/lite

light: Illumination from the sun, stars, fire, or a light bulb (natural **light** from the sun is better for you than sitting inside all day); used also to describe various forms of light [e.g., traffic **light**, gas**light**]; colloquial: to give permission (you have been given the **green light** to go ahead with your appeal); to fully understand a situation (she was quick to see the **light** and gave the correct answer); used detrimentally, to describe someone who is stupid or useless (the **light** is on but no one is at home); also the opposite to heavy in terms of weight (she is quite **light** so I can easily pick her up); colloquial: to indicate lacking substance (he is only a **light**weight, so you should appeal to someone with more authority)

lite: Colloquial term referring to the use or content of less of a substance usually by food manufacturers (**lite** milk has less fat than full-cream milk)

lightening/lightning

lightening: To lessen or diminish (the decision to hire an apprentice had the effect of **lightening** my workload; my concerns about my children are **lightening** now that they both have secured good jobs); changing to a lighter hue (**lightening** my hair from dull brown to blonde has made me feel more attractive)

lightning: A flash of light caused by an electrical discharge in the atmosphere (you need to be careful not to be out in the open or under a tree when **lightning** strikes); colloquial: used to indicate something that should not happen again (**lightning**

never strikes the same place twice!); colloquial: indicating high speed (he runs fast like **lightning**)

lightning/lightening (see lightening/lightning)

links/lynx

> **links:** The rings or separate circles that form into a bracelet or wristband (Barbara had to take her watch back to the jeweler to have one of the **links** removed); to have a connection with something or someone (Eric still has **links** with his former regiment); to join together (she **links** her arms around Mark's neck when she kisses him)

> **lynx:** A wildcat with long legs and a short tail (the **lynx** is found in Canada and the northern United States)

lite/light (see light/lite)

llama/lama (see lama/llama)

lo/low

> **lo:** To attract attention to something, used mainly in the expression "**Lo and behold**," which appears in many texts in the King James Bible, as well as in many hymns

> **low:** The opposite of high, meaning to be shorter or nearer to the ground or the floor (he is erecting his tent on the **low** ground); to have no greatness or expectations (he is only **low** on the corporate ladder); to be thought of as despicable (he has such a **low** character, I wouldn't trust him); to be depressed (I feel so **low** today, I can hardly get out of bed); to be soft or quiet (he talks in such a **low** voice, it is hard

to hear him); a musical term meaning a quiet or soft tone (this piece is sung in a **low** pitch); in weather, regions of rising air that often bring clouds and rain (the **low** pressure system is likely to affect the weather tomorrow)

load/lode/lowed

load: Something that is laid or put into a vehicle to be conveyed elsewhere (he had a **load** of furniture that he had to move to the new house); the action of laying goods to be conveyed (he needs to **load** the truck quickly before the rain starts); to arm a gun or put film in a camera (he had to **load** his camera before he took any shots); burden (he was bearing the **load** of her grief); colloquial: to be relieved from (it was **a load off his mind** when he saw he had enough money in the bank to pay his debts)

lode: An amount of a mineral that fills a space in rock

lowed: The past tense of "to low," which means to moo

loan/lone

loan: Something that you allow someone to borrow (my car is on **loan** to Dan for the weekend); goods you have for a specific period before a penalty is incurred (this book is on **loan** from the library until Wednesday); an amount of money obtained from a bank (the monthly payment for the **loan** on our house is due on the 14th of each month)

lone: Solitary or only one (it is the **lone** tree standing after the storm)

loch/lock

loch: A lake that is almost completely surrounded by land (**Loch** Ness in Scotland is famous for the Loch Ness monster)

lock: To secure (I need to **lock** the door before I go out); the device to secure something (I have a safety **lock** on each door); a small piece of hair (I keep a **lock** of my daughter's hair in my locket); colloquial: part of the expression to mean everything (I have sold the house, **lock, stock and barrel**)

lochs/locks/lox

lochs: The plural of "loch" (Scotland has a great number of **lochs**, including Loch Lomond, Loch Ness, and Loch Maree)

locks: A form of the verb "to lock" and the plural of the noun "lock"; to secure (the guard **locks** the gate every night to prevent anyone from entering); devices used to make things secure (there are so many **locks** on the doors in this house that it would take someone hours to break in); refers to hair (many people comment on her beautiful **locks**)

lox: A kind of brine-cured salmon (I prefer to eat my bagel with cream cheese and **lox**)

lock/loch (see loch/lock)

locks/lox/lochs (see lochs/locks/lox)

lode/lowed/load (see load/lode/lowed)

lone/loan (see loan/lone)

loot/lute

> **loot:** Anything that is taken dishonestly, usually referring to the proceeds of a burglary (he stored the **loot** that he had taken from the jewelry shop in his garage)

> **lute:** A stringed musical instrument with a vaulted back and pear-shaped body (the **lute** was very popular during the medieval and renaissance periods, though some lutes are still being made and played today)

low/lo (see lo/low)

lowed/load/lode (see load/lode/lowed)

lox/lochs/locks (see lochs/locks/lox)

lumbar/lumber

> **lumbar:** Relates to the loin area, the lower part of the back (after his accident he had considerable pain in the **lumbar** region in the fifth vertebrae)

> **lumber:** Timber that has been sawn into pieces (after they had finished sawing, they had to load the **lumber** on trucks to take to the factory); a description of moving heavily and clumsily (with my full-leg cast, I **lumber** about the house, making a lot of noise and bumping into furniture)

lumber/lumbar (see lumbar/lumber)

lute/loot (see loot/lute)

lye/lie (see lie/lye)

lynx/links (see links/lynx)

lyre/liar (see liar/lyre)

≳ M ≲

made/maid

made: The past tense and past participle of the verb "to make" (she has **made** her best sponge cake ever and should win the prize); succeeded or was successful (the team **made** it to the semifinals of the competition); colloquial: to be fortunate or wealthy (they **have it made**); colloquial: to be suited (they were **made** for each other)

maid: A young unmarried girl or a spinster (Felicity is an **old maid**); a person who does household duties for payment (they have such a big house, they needed to hire a **maid** to help clean and cook)

maid/made (see made/maid)

mail/male

mail: Letters and packages posted and either delivered or collected (I just heard the mailman drop today's **mail** in our mailbox); a common expression by someone who has defaulted on a payment (**the check is in the mail**); a coat of armor made of interlaced rings or chains (the wearing of **chain mail** and body armor dates back to the Greeks and early Roman Empire)

male: In the human species, the result of the union of X and Y sex chromosomes during sexual intercourse or in-vitro fertilization (according to the Bible, Adam was the first **male** born in the world)

main/Maine/mane

main: The principal or most important part of an event, conference, book, etc. (the **main** point of the article was the introduction of measures to eliminate nuclear warfare); the most important person, sportsperson, actor, etc. at an event or in a performance (the **main** speaker at the conference received great applause); an expression meaning "for the most part" (**in the main** we have received considerable support from the politicians)

Maine: A state of the United States of America (**Maine** became the 23rd state of the United States on March 15, 1820)

mane: The long hair on the back and shoulders of animals, such as lions, tigers, and horses; figuratively, can refer to long, untidy hair of humans (Josh, are you ever going to get that **mane** of hair cut?)

Maine/mane/main (see main/Maine/mane)

maize/maze

maize: A cultivated cereal crop also known as corn

maze: A network of confusing interconnected pathways or passages (every Halloween we go to the corn **maze** at the haunted house) male/mail (see mail/male)

mall/maul

    mall: A shopping complex (the shopping **mall** was designed to attract shoppers into the city); a shaded walk (the **mall** in St James Park leading to Buckingham Place is very popular with foreign visitors)

    maul: A heavy hammer used for driving in stakes, piles, or wedges; to savage with teeth, claws by an animal (they were warned not to go too close to the dog, as it could **maul** them)

mane/main/Maine (see main/Maine/mane)

manner/manor

    manner: The way in which something is done or a particular mode of action (it has always been our **manner** to have roast lamb on Sunday); one's behavior when in the company of others (he acted in the **manner** of someone much older)

    manor: A landed estate (in medieval times, the lord of the **manor** controlled all woodlands, cottages, etc. in his estate); also a large stately home

manor/manner (see manner/manor)

mantel/mantle

    mantel: The shelf over a fireplace (she has many photos on the **mantel**)

mantle: A long, sleeveless cloak that covers the shoulders, etc.; something that covers or conceals (he was covered by the **mantle** of darkness)

mantle/mantel (see mantel/mantle)

mark/marque

mark: A visible dent or impression (he held her arm so strongly that it left a **mark** on her skin); a symbol used in writing or printing (Keith was prone to overuse the exclamation **mark**); a number or symbol indicating a level of success (Helena received an excellent **mark** of A+ for her essay); the object of aim (in your first attempt you were off the **mark**); colloquial: a person whom a swindler has picked out (he decided that the young inexperienced man would be a good **mark**); colloquial: to misunderstand (he was way **off the mark** when he thought I was insulting his companion)

marque: The brand name of a product, particularly the emblem of a car (although **marque** is rarely used today, there still are Marque Car Associations with large numbers of affiliates)

marque/mark (see mark/marque)

marshal/martial

marshal: A high-ranking officer in some armed forces; a federal law enforcement agent; a person who arranges and directs the ceremonial aspects of a gathering (he was the grand **marshal** of the parade for the fifth year in a row)

martial: Rule by military authorities, usually temporary, imposed on a civilian population in wartime (**martial law** can also be imposed when a ruling party is threatened by popular protest); also describes various systematized methods of self-defense (**martial** arts originated in China, Korea, and Japan and later spread throughout the rest of the world)

martial/marshal (see marshal/martial)

mask/masque

mask: A covering of the face, mainly to disguise (Julie wore a **mask** to the ball hoping she would not be recognized); a covering of the face as protection against dust, smoke, potential viruses, etc. (in Tokyo it is common to see people on the street wearing a **mask**); protection against gas, particularly during wars (during both world wars, people were issued with a gas **mask**)

masque: A masked ball (the word **masque** comes from "masquerade": to wear a mask to conceal); a form of dramatic entertainment popular among the English aristocracy during the 16th and 17th centuries, when the entertainment included lavish costumes, music, scenery, and dancing

masque/mask (see mask/masque)

mat/matte

mat: A piece of fabric or woven fibers such as straw, hemp, or similar used on a floor or doorstep (Zac, please wipe your dirty shoes on the **mat** before you enter the house); a small strip or square of cotton, linen, or cardboard used to place under a dish or plate on a table or under a vase (a place**mat** under a hot dish is very useful to protect a dining table from damage)

matte: Dull, not shiny, finish on metals, paint, and photographic paper (many photographers prefer a **matte** rather than gloss finish on photographs)

matte/mat (see mat/matte)

maul/mall (see mall/maul)

maze/maize (see maize/maze)

me/mi

me: Personal pronoun, the objective case of "I" (would you please pass **me** the salt?)

mi: In music, part of a scale [e.g., do, re, **mi**, fa, so, la, ti]

mean/mien

mean: To intend, to have in mind (I did **mean** to talk to the doctor about that rash but forgot); to explain the intention (what I did **mean** was that schools should ensure that no child is ever bullied); being miserly (he is so **mean**, he probably has the first dollar he ever earned); colloquial: powerful (that car is a **mean** machine); to be cruel (stop being so **mean** to your sister!)

mien: Bearing, appearance (he portrays the **mien** of a successful businessman: confident and commanding)

meat/meet

meat: Flesh of an animal used for food (our family has roast **meat** every Sunday)

meet: To come in contact with, or to make a connection (Jane has agreed to **meet** Sarah at the movies); to greet (Ruby will **meet** her guests at the foyer); to compromise (we will **meet** halfway); colloquial: to die (he will shortly **meet his maker**)

medal/meddle

medal: A small symbol recognizing bravery or service, particularly in armed forces, sporting achievements, etc. (the lieutenant received a **medal** for saving a member of his platoon while under fire; he was awarded a **medal** for bravery after rescuing several children from drowning)

meddle: To interfere or busy oneself (she is known to **meddle** in matters that are not her concern)

meddle/medal (see medal/meddle)

meet/ meat (see meat/meet)

metal/mettle

metal: An elementary substance, such as gold, silver, iron, copper, lead, tin, and alloys of aluminum, copper, etc. (silver is a **metal** that requires constant cleaning, particularly silver cutlery)

mettle: Strength of a person's character (to run the marathon, he displayed considerable **mettle**); showing courage (it took a lot of **mettle** to dive into that flooded river to save those people)

mettle/metal (see metal/mettle)

mewl/mule

mewl: The cry of a cat or the whimper of a young child (the **mewl** of the cat kept us awake last night)

mule: The sterile offspring of a female horse and a male donkey (the **mule** is used as a beast of burden as it is patient and surefooted); colloquial: to indicate a person who is very obstinate or stupid (he is a stubborn **mule** and won't do anything he is asked to do); a name for a type of slipper that doesn't cover the heel

mi/me (see me/mi)

mien/mean (see mean/mien)

might/mite

might: Expressing uncertainty (I **might** have to move to another area to find work); referring to an event contrary to what happened (the nuclear disaster after the earthquake **might** have turned out much worse); a tentative suggestion (we **might** go to the movies next Saturday); power or strength (the **might** of the ocean can sometimes be frightening)

mite: A small insect, often parasitic, living on plants and animals; also a biblical reference to the donation by a widow who gave what money she could, known as the widow's **mite**; colloquial: a small child

mince/mints

mince: To cut or chop meat into very small pieces (the recipe says we need to **mince**, not chop, the onion); to soften your words (she would very carefully **mince** her words to avoid giving offense)

mints: The plural of "mint," a sweet that can be chewed or sucked (she offered **mints** to all her friends); colloquial: to be rich (Richard has made a **mint**)

mind/mined

mind: The part of the brain that is associated with perception, thinking, purpose, memory, emotions, and thoughts (in my **mind** I am working out ways to complete my project on time); someone considered to have great intellect (Stephen Hawkins is a brilliant **mind**); to remember (you need to keep in **mind** your appointment with the doctor); to be careful (**mind** how you cross the road); to look after someone or something (would you please **mind** my cat while I go on vacation?); to be cautious (**mind** what you say in front of the children)

mined: The past tense of the verb "to mine," meaning to excavate (they **mined** for gold without any success)

mined/mind (see mind/mined)

miner/minor

miner: Someone who digs in a mine (Harry has been a coal **miner** since he was 15 years old); also a bird of the honeyeater family that has a yellow beak and yellow/brown legs (a bellbird is classified as a **miner**)

minor: A person who is under the legal age (it is a criminal offense to have sex with a **minor**); of little importance (it is only a **minor** offense, not worthy of pursuing)

minor/miner (see miner/minor)

mints/mince (see mince/mints)

missed/mist

missed: The past tense of the verb "to miss," meaning failed to hit, obtain, accomplish, etc. (that car just **missed** hitting the little girl; I **missed** out on winning first place in the race); to fail to hear, perceive, or understand (I **missed** out on what the speaker was saying as there was too much noise in the room)

mist: A light fog or haze (be careful, as there is a light **mist** and you could easily fall); blurring of vision (I have a **mist** over my eyes and can hardly see)

mist/missed (see missed/mist)

mite/might (see might/mite)

moan/mown

moan: A long, low, mournful sound associated with grief or suffering (the widow's **moan** at the funeral was pitiful to hear); colloquial: to complain (she is known to **moan** about everything)

mown: The past participle of the verb "to mow," meaning to cut grass, grain, etc. with a mower or scythe (it is always pleasant to see a freshly **mown** lawn)

moat/mote

moat: A wide, deep trench usually filled with water surrounding a town, castle, or house (he swam the **moat** hoping to gain access to the castle without being seen)

mote: A small speck, especially of dust (he had a **mote** of dust in his eye)

mode/mowed

mode: A method or way of expressing (the music was written in the **mode** of Mozart); a camera setting (to take the shot of the man running, he set the digital camera in action **mode**); a style or fashion (she was dressed in the **mode** of the 1930s for the fancy dress ball)

mowed: Past tense of the verb "to mow" (I **mowed** the lawn yesterday)

mood/mooed

mood: A particular frame of mind (he was in a foul **mood**, muttering to himself and being thoroughly irritable)

mooed: The past tense of the verb "to moo" (as soon as the cow **mooed**, we knew it was time to milk her)

mooed/mood (see mood/mooed)

moose/mousse

moose: A large deer with antlers, a sloping back, and a growth of skin hanging from the neck (the **moose**

is found in northern Eurasia and northern North America)

mousse: A dessert of whipped cream, beaten eggs, and gelatin in various flavors (strawberry **mousse** is my favorite dessert); a substance used for setting or styling hair (many boys use **mousse** to make their hair stiff and stand upright)

morning/mourning

morning: The beginning of the day; the time between dawn and noon (it was a beautiful sunny **morning** so we decided to go for a picnic; we made a decision to work only in the **morning** hours and each afternoon go swimming)

mourning: Grieving, lamenting (we are all **mourning** the loss of our brother, who was killed in an accident)

mote/moat (see moat/mote)

mourning/morning (see morning/mourning)

mousse/moose (see moose/mousse)

mowed/mode (see mode/mowed)

mown/moan (see moan/mown)

mule/mewl (see mewl/mule)

muscles/mussels

muscles: Contractile fibers that enable the body to move (the body needs **muscles** for each movement

of the arm, legs, etc.); colloquial: political power
or strength (he has the **muscle** to achieve this
amalgamation); colloquial: to interfere sometimes
using force (she will **muscle** her way in and take over
using whatever means it takes)

mussels: Bivalve mollusks with a double-hinged shell
found in both fresh and saltwater; also known as clams
(**mussels** are my favorite seafood dish)

mussels/muscles (see muscles/mussels)

mustard/mustered

mustard: A pungent paste or powder used as a
condiment or flavoring (would you like **mustard** or
mayonnaise on your ham sandwich?)

mustered: Past tense of "to muster," meaning to
assemble troops, flight or sea crews, etc. for inspection,
special duties, displays (the troops were **mustered**,
ready to attack the enemy at dawn); colloquial: to
gather or summon (the officer **mustered** all his strength
to carry the wounded soldier and get him to safety)

mustered/mustard (see mustard/mustered)

≥ N ≤

naval/navel

naval: Referring to the navy [e.g., ships, personnel,
bases, stores, etc.] (the newly appointed **naval**
commander will inspect the **naval** base today)

navel: The depression in the center of the stomach, the umbilicus (**navel** piercing has become very popular with young girls)

nave/knave (see knave/nave)

navel/naval (see naval/navel)

nay/neigh

nay: Archaic form of "no," meaning refusal, denial, or dissent, mainly used in meetings to indicate a negative vote (the result of the count is 40 ayes and one **nay**)

neigh: The sound made by a horse, a whinny (the horse's **neigh** is a way of attracting attention similar to a dog's bark)

need/knead/kneed (see knead/kneed/need)

neigh/nay (see nay/neigh)

new/gnu/knew (see gnu/knew/new)

night/knight (see knight/night)

nit/knit (see knit/nit)

no/know (see know/no)

nob/knob (see knob/nob)

noes/nose/knows (see knows/noes/nose)

none/nun

> **none:** No one, not one (I waited for a letter from my mother but **none** came); nothing (there is **none** available at the present time)

> **nun:** A woman who lives in a convent and has taken a vow of chastity and obedience (Sister Genevieve has been a **nun** at St. Mary's Convent for the past 20 years)

nose/knows/noes (see knows/noes/nose)

not/knot (see knot/not)

nun/none (see none/nun)

≳ O ≲

oar/or/ore

> **oar:** An instrument used to row a boat (Michael had only one **oar** to steer the boat)

> **or:** A conjunction used to indicate alternatives (black **or** white)

> **ore:** A rock or mineral bearing ore [e.g., iron **ore**]

ode/owed

> **ode:** A lyrical poem originally intended to be sung (poet John Keats wrote **Ode to a Nightingale** in May 1819)

> **owed:** An amount to be repaid (Simon is **owed** $1,000 for the carpentry work he did on his friend's house);

colloquial: to be in debt to (he **owed** his friend his thanks for supporting him through his divorce)

oh/owe

oh: An exclamation of surprise, sorrow, pain, pleasure, or for attracting attention (**oh**, what a beautiful engagement ring; **oh**, that hurt!)

owe: To be in debt (I still **owe** Nancy money for the theatre tickets); to be obligated to pay or repay (I **owe** a debt of loyalty to my sister for all the support she has given me)

one/won

one: A cardinal number as the symbol 1; a depiction of this number of items (**one** orange); a single person or thing, or an individual instance (there is only **one** way to hold a knife and fork); to indicate unity (we are all **at one** regarding what happened); indicating how traffic must travel (this is a **one**-way street); colloquial: to be fixated or focused on something (you really do have a **one-track mind**!)

won: To be victorious; to be first in a race or competition (Jeff **won** the freestyle race at the state swimming finals); to gain or persuade (the developer **won** the bid for the project)

or/ore/oar (see oar/or/ore)

oracle/auricle (see auricle/oracle)

oral/aural (see aural/oral)

ore/oar/or (see oar/or/ore)

our/hour (see hour/our)

overseas/oversees

    overseas: To be abroad (Hilary is traveling **overseas** for two months); adjective describing "foreign" (he has two months left of **overseas** service)

    oversees: Supervises or keeps watch over (the factory manager **oversees** the daily work routine to ensure that all orders are completed on time)

oversees/overseas (see overseas/oversees)

owe/oh (see oh/owe)

owed/ode (see ode/owed)

⋛ P ⋚

paced/paste

    paced: Rate of stepping or movement (he **paced** up and down the room waiting for the doctor to finish his wife's surgery)

    paste: A mixture of flour and water used for sticking paper (children love to make a **paste** so they can place pictures from magazines onto paper); any material in a soft mass [e.g., tooth**paste**]

packed/pact

packed: Past tense of "to pack," meaning to assemble items, clothes, etc. (I have **packed** the suitcase for our trip); colloquial: stopped or ceased (they **packed it in** after training all day); colloquial: crammed (they were all **packed like sardines** into the subway car)

pact: An agreement, a compact (we made a **pact** not to argue for the whole day; the NATO nations made a **pact** to intervene in the war in northern Africa)

pact/packed (see packed/pact)

pail/pale

pail: A bucket; any cylindrical container with a hooped handle suitable for carrying substances (in the nursery rhyme, Jack and Jill went up the hill to fetch a **pail** of water)

pale: Lacking color (her face was **pale** without makeup); of a light hue (she wore a **pale** blue dress to the function); feeble (he made a **pale** attempt to stop the argument); less important (it was a **pale** imitation of the real painting); colloquial: to do something not morally or socially acceptable (what he did to that animal was **beyond the pale**)

pain/pane

pain: Agony, discomfort, suffering in the body or mind (she was groaning, clutching her ankle and obviously in considerable **pain**; colloquial: a nuisance (he is just a **pain in the neck**); to be extremely careful (she is **at pains** to not make an error)

pane: A section of a window (the children were playing baseball and broke a **pane** of glass in the neighbor's window)

pair/pare/pear

pair: Two of anything (a **pair** of trousers is so named because the trousers have two legs); two parts that are joined together (a **pair** of scissors); in playing cards when you have two cards of the same value (I have a **pair** of queens and a **pair** of eights, and that beats your one **pair** of kings)

pare: To cut off the outer covering or coating (I will **pare** an apple for you as long as you eat it all); to reduce in size (you need to **pare down** your estimate, or you will not get the job)

pear: A piece of edible fruit (the **pear** is a very popular fruit, usually eaten raw); colloquial: to describe a particular body shape (it is difficult to find suitable clothes when you are **pear** shaped)

palate/palette/pallet

palate: The roof of the mouth, consisting of a hard **palate**, the bony area in front, and a soft **palate**, the fleshy area at the back (Sarah has a high **palate** called a cathedral **palate** as a result of being born with Marfan syndrome); a person's appreciation of taste and flavor (she has a refined **palate** for good wine)

palette: A board used by painters to mix paints (her **palette** is a circular board with a hole at one end for the thumb)

pallet: A platform that allows bricks, wood, etc. to be placed on it ready to be raised by a forklift truck and transported (I ordered a **pallet** of bricks to be delivered on Wednesday); also a flat blade with a handle used by potters (the **pallet** is an essential tool for shaping pots)

pale/pail (see pail/pale)

palette/pallet/palate (see palate/palette/pallet)

pallet/palate/palette (see palate/palette/pallet)

pane/pain (see pain/pane)

pare/pear/pair (see pair/pare/pear)

passed/past

passed: Past tense of "to pass," meaning to overtake, to go by (as he was a fast runner, he **passed** the other competitors without much effort); crossed over (she **passed** over the bridge to get to the road); succeeded (Angus **passed** his mathematics exam with flying colors); colloquial: died (he **passed over** to the other side)

past: Something that happened or existed some time ago (we don't remember who caused the argument, because it's all in the **past**); a grammatical term denoting the tenses of verbs that refer to actions already completed; to be out of date (these tablets are **past** their use-by date)

past/passed (see passed/past)

paste/paced (see paced/paste)

patience/patients

patience: Uncomplaining, waiting without getting annoyed, calmness (I am amazed at her **patience,** as she never complains when she is kept waiting to be served)

patients: People who are being attended to by a doctor, physiotherapist, dentist, etc. (the office is always crowded because he is a popular doctor with a large number of **patients**)

patients/patience (see patience/patients)

pause/paws

pause: A temporary stop, particularly in action or speech (I often **pause** when I am speaking, sometimes for effect but often because I can't remember what I was going to say; sometimes when I am mowing a large lawn, I **pause** to have a glass of water); also a musical symbol placed over or below a note to indicate a **pause**

paws: The feet of animals with claws and nails (I need special nail cutters to trim my dog's **paws**); colloquial: a human hand (keep your dirty **paws** off me)

paws/pause (see pause/paws)

peace/piece

peace: The end of hostilities between countries (there was **peace** in Europe after Germany surrendered to the Allies in May 1945 ending World War II); freedom from strife (once they agreed on sharing the household duties, there was **peace** in the home); freedom from mental upset (I have some **peace of mind** now that I have paid off the loan); a state of calm (I love the **peace** in the house when everyone is out); to remain quiet (she held her **peace** and listened without interruption)

piece: A small amount of something (I would like a **piece** of cake); one of a smaller division of a block (could you break off a **piece** of chocolate for me, please); any part of a jigsaw puzzle or a board game (I think this **piece** can be placed there to complete the house in the puzzle); to describe an individual work or composition (this table is a fine **piece** of genuine oak); colloquial: a firearm (this **piece** was the gun used in the robbery)

peak/peek/pique

peak: The top of a mountain (at long last we have reached the **peak**); an identifying landmark (we know we are near our destination when we see a **peak** on the right); the highest point (the tide will **peak** at 10 a.m.); description of a way hair grows (she tries to comb her hair so as to disguise her widow's **peak**)

peek: To look at something secretly (he would often **peek** from his window at the girls walking past); to view something quickly (come and have a quick **peek** at the house for sale)

pique: A feeling of annoyance or irritation (I felt a moment of **pique** when she wrongly accused me)

peal/peel

peal: The sound of bells ringing (the church bells **peal** every hour); an outburst of sound (Kate shudders every time she hears a **peal** of thunder)

peel: To strip off an outer covering (the bark on that tree will soon start to **peel**); to lose skin (I hate it when I start to **peel** after being sunburned)

pear/pair/pare (see pair/pare/pear)

pearl/purl

pearl: A hard, lustrous nacreous concretion formed within the shell of bivalve mollusks such as oysters, commonly used in jewelry (she was given a beautiful **pearl** ring for her birthday); colloquial: something special (she is a **pearl** of a secretary); a pale color similar to the luster of a pearl (she wore a beautiful **pearl**-colored gown to the wedding)

purl: A knitting stitch (Susan knitted her first jumper in **purl** and plain)

pedal/peddle

pedal: A foot lever on a piano, organ, sewing machine, or machinery (you depress this **pedal** on the right to play the piano softly); the action of using a pedal (you will need to **pedal** fast on your bicycle if you want to get to school on time)

peddle: To trade or sell (the old man will often **peddle** his wares door to door) peddle/pedal (see pedal/peddle)

peek/pique/peak (see peak/peek/pique)

peel/peal (see peal/peel)

peer/pier

> **peer:** A person who is your equal in status (he is my **peer** in academic status, as we both have PhDs in modern history and lecture at the university); to look narrowly or earnestly (he often would **peer** at the stars at night); a group of people of the same age, social group, occupation, etc. (the **peer group** he belongs to is aged 15 to 17)

> **pier:** A wooden structure extending from the shore into the sea; a wharf (the well-known tourist attraction Brighton **Pier** is less than an hour by train from London)

per/purr

> **per:** Through, by means of, for each (the letter is signed by the manager, **per** his secretary; the gas today is $2.49 **per** gallon)

> **purr:** The low, contented sound made by a cat

phase/faze (see faze/phase)

phew/few (see few/phew)

phial/file (see file/phial)

phishing/fishing (see fishing/phishing)

phlox/flocks (see flocks/phlox)

phrase/frays (see frays/phrase)

pi/pie

pi: The 16th letter of the Greek alphabet; representation of the symbol for the ratio of the circumference of a circle to its diameter in math

pie: A dish of fruit, meat, or vegetables covered with pastry and baked in an oven (apple **pie** with ice cream is my favorite dessert)

pidgin/pigeon

pidgin: A non-specific language used for communication between various groups having different first languages (**pidgin** English was first used as a means of communication between the English and the Chinese in the 19th century)

pigeon: A bird similar to a dove (the homing **pigeon** was used as military messengers in World War II)

pie/pi (see pi/pie)

piece/peace (see peace/piece)

pier/peer (see peer/pier)

pigeon/pidgin (see pidgin/pigeon)

pique/peak/peek (see peak/peek/pique)

plain/plane

plain: Unadorned or uncluttered (I have decided on a **plain** white dress with no frills or bows for my wedding dress); clear and easy to hear or understand (he used **plain**, simple language to help us understand the situation); downright (the message was **plain** and direct); not beautiful (her mother called her "**plain** Jane and no nonsense"); flat, level country (the **plain** seemed to stretch as far as the eye could see)

plane: A flat or level surface; a level of existence, character, etc. (he lives on a higher **plane** than the rest of us); the shortened form of "airplane" (our **plane** is due to arrive at noon); a tool resembling a plaster trowel used for leveling the clay in a brick mould; also a tool used by carpenters for leveling a piece of wood

plane/plain (see plain/plane)

pleas/please

pleas: Appeals for mercy, leniency, help, etc. (Cheryl's **pleas** for help were heard by the people in the street); suits or actions in law (the **pleas** of innocence were rejected by the court)

please: To give pleasure (I hope this birthday present will **please** him); a polite request (could you **please** pass the salt and pepper?); to find something to your liking (choose whatever you **please** from the menu)

please/pleas (see pleas/please)

plum/plumb

plum: A fruit related to the cherry (it is difficult to choose between strawberry and **plum** jam); a color or hue (**plum** is a popular color for prom dresses); colloquial: something good (Jenny has a **plum** job)

plumb: A small weight of lead or similar attached to a string to ensure something is completely vertical or horizontal (John had to use a **plumb** line to ensure that the fence was completely level)

plumb/plum (see plum/plumb)

pole/poll

pole: A long, rounded piece of wood used for various purposes (you need to have the **pole** straight when you erect the tent; you often see a car crashed into a telegraph **pole**)

poll: Votes cast in an election (the national **poll** to elect a new president will close at 8 p.m.); to assess public opinion (a **poll** has been taken on the numbers in favor of legalizing marijuana)

poll/pole (see pole/poll)

poor/pore/pour

poor: Having very little money or very few possessions (they are so **poor** they are unable to buy enough food to feed the family); having limited skills or insight (his writing is so **poor** that he will never be able to pass a written examination); countries lacking resources or funds (Third World countries are **poor** and need assistance from richer nations); inferior goods, health, etc. (his health is **poor**); adjective describing a person to be pitied (the **poor** woman lost both her sons in a car accident)

pore: To gaze at or read intently (he will often **pore** over his manuscript); to meditate or review (it is her practice to **pore over** the actions she took to remedy the situation); a minute opening on the skin or on a leaf for absorption (when you are extremely hot, you perspire from every **pore**)

pour: To send a liquid or loose flakes falling or flowing into a bowl or container (you need to **pour** the milk onto your cereal); to rain heavily (make certain you get home before it starts to **pour**); colloquial: to talk as in a stream (don't get him started on the economy or it will all **pour out**)

populace/populous

populace: The common mass of the population (the **populace** is in opposition to the new measures taken by the government)

populous: Well-populated (China is a **populous** country)

populous/populace (see populace/populous)

pore/pour/poor (see poor/pore/pour)

pores/pours

pores: Present tense of "to pore," meaning to gaze at or read intently (he **pores** over the newspaper every morning); reviews or meditates (Susan **pores over** the shopping list to ensure every item they need is listed); the minute openings on the skin or on a leaf for absorption (without a magnifying glass it would be difficult to see the **pores** on your skin)

pours: Similar to "pour," the action of sending loose flakes or a liquid falling or flowing into a bowl or container (when she **pours** water from the watering can, she drowns the flowers); rains heavily (it always **pours** just when I hang my towels on the line to dry); talking in a stream (when you ask how her marriage is, her unhappiness with her situation in life **pours** out)

pour/ poor/pore (see poor/pore/pour)

pours/pores (see pores/pours)

praise/prays/preys

praise: To commend, laud, or extol (it is important to **praise** children for their efforts)

prays: Beseeches or requests (she **prays** for mercy from her tormentor); in a religious context (the child **prays** to God every night)

preys: Exerts unhealthy or harmful influence (the blackmailer **preys** on his victims); the plural of "prey," which refers to below, animals hunted for food

pray/prey

pray: To beseech or to request (I will **pray** for your soul; farmers **pray** for rain)

prey: An animal hunted for food (hunters use guns or spears to kill their **prey**); a person or thing that falls victim to an enemy or disease (he fell **prey** to cholera after ministering to the ill)

prays/preys/praise (see praise/prays/preys)

precedence/precedents

precedence: Pride of place or priority of order (applications received by the due date have **precedence** over late submissions)

precedents: Previous examples of some actions or rulings, particularly used in law (the **precedents** in this case give sufficient justification for the prosecution's case to be thrown out)

precedents/precedence (see precedence/precedents)

presence/presents

presence: The act of being there to witness something (his **presence** at the wedding was totally unexpected); description of someone's demeanor or bearing (the mayor has such an impressive **presence** that everyone listens to him)

presents: Gifts (kids love opening their **presents** on Christmas Day)

presents/presence (see presence/presents)

prey/pray (see pray/prey)

preys/praise/prays (see praise/prays/preys)

pride/pried

pride: Overwhelming sense or opinion of one's importance, achievements, dignity, or superiority (Ken announced with **pride** that he had made his first million dollars at the age of 20); a personal sense of achievement (Paul took **pride** in having a clean, polished car); the name of a company of lions

pried: Past tense of the verb "to peer," meaning to spy or to look at closely (the company **pried** into the affairs of its employees)

pried/pride (see pride/pried)

pries/ prize

pries: Peers, spies, or looks at closely (she is upset when her girlfriend **pries** into her affairs)

prize: An award for effort, academic results, winning a race, etc. (the **prize** for first place in the scholarship competition was a $100 gift certificate); something that is valued (her **prize** possession was the car given to her by her parents for her 18th birthday)

prince/prints

prince: The son or grandson of a king or queen (**Prince** William is the grandson of Queen Elizabeth II of Great Britain); someone who commands respect (he is the **prince** of peace)

prints: Produces a photo, newspaper, etc. (Ron **prints** his digital photos although most people just store them on the computer); writes in letters rather than in cursive strokes (Susan's handwriting is so illegible, she **prints** the names on her invitation cards instead); colloquial: fingerprints (his **prints** are all over the place); another name for photographs (photos are often referred to as **prints**)

principal/principle

principal: A person of importance or rank (he is the **principal** organizer of the event); a person who takes the leading role in a performance (she is the **principal** dancer in the musical); a sum of money on which interest is charged (the **principal** owed to the bank is approximately $100,000); in law, a person who is directly responsible for a crime (Joe Simmonds is the **principal** offender in the murder of his brother)

principle: A fundamental element, or an accepted rule of action or conduct (democracy is based on the **principle** of one man, one vote); according to the rule generally followed (we have made an agreement **in principle**)

principle/principal (see principal/principle)

prints/prince (see prince/prints)

prize/pries (see pries/prize)

profit/prophet

profit: The gain made after subtracting expenses from the money received in business transactions (I made a **profit** on the deal to supply tents for the festival); individual, non-financial gain (he will certainly **profit** from learning music from a master)

prophet: A person who foretells the future (many who profess to be a **prophet** will foretell when the world will end); someone who speaks as the messenger of God or is regarded as a great teacher (Isaiah is the most quoted **prophet** in the New Testament of the Bible)

prophet/profit (see profit/prophet)

pros/prose

pros: An abbreviation of "professionals" (they are **pros**, so let them get on with the job); also arguments in favor of a proposal (we have listened to the **pros** and cons, so we will now put it to the vote)

prose: The ordinary way of writing, such as in a novel or newspaper, as distinct from poetry or verse (his **prose** could certainly be improved)

prose/pros (see pros/prose)

purl/pearl (see pearl/purl)

purr/per (see per/purr)

≳ Q ≲

quarts/quartz

quarts: The plural of "quart," a measure of volume equal to a quarter of a gallon, 2 pints, or 4 cups (average-sized pitchers make 2 **quarts** of iced tea)

quartz: A crystalline rock having many varieties that differ in color, luster, size, etc. (an amethyst is one form of **quartz**); also used in watchmaking (the **quartz** crystal ensures great accuracy in a watch or clock)

quartz/quarts (see quarts/quartz)

quay/cay/key (see cay/key/quay)

queue/cue (see cue/queue)

quire/choir (see choir/quire)

≳ R ≴

racket/racquet

racket: A loud noise or uproar (the children were making such a **racket** that we couldn't hear the television); an organized, illegal moneymaking scheme (extorting protection money from small businesses is a **racket**); a suspect scheme to gain money (it's a **racket** the way the stores put up their prices and then reduce them in a sale)

racquet: A light bat with an elliptical frame and strings of nylon or cord used in badminton, tennis, or squash (some tennis players in frustration smash their **racquet** on the court)

racquet/racket (see racket/racquet)

rain/reign/rein

rain: The condensation of vapor in the atmosphere that falls in drops to the earth (we hope for **rain** when there is a drought); to indicate a number of blows in a fight (his practice was to **rain** blows quickly on his opponents); colloquial: to indicate heavy rain (hurry inside because it is just about to **rain cats and dogs**)

reign: The period of time a king or queen rules a country (Queen Victoria's **reign** over England lasted for nearly 64 years, from 1837 to 1901); the length of time anyone exerts influence in an organization or similar (the **reign** of a CEO of any business organization lasts until he either resigns, retires, or is ousted); used colloquially to indicate authority (Ken's mother **reigns** over the household)

rein: A long, narrow strip of leather attached to the bridle of a horse that allows the rider to control the actions of the horse (you must make certain to hold the **reins** tightly when riding); to restrict or restrain (you must **rein in** your temper); to give complete license or scope (you have **free rein** to organize the luncheon as you wish)

raise/rays/raze

raise: To lift or elevate (you need to **raise** your hand to indicate that you are for the motion); to erect (the people have decided to **raise** a monument to commemorate those who died in the rescue attempt); to cultivate (we will **raise** wheat and corn in these fields); to bring up children (she was asked to **raise** her brother's children when he and his wife died); to collect (the community decided to **raise** funds to help those who lost everything in the flood); to increase prices, wages, or rates (the bank decided to **raise** its interest rate); colloquial: to cause a commotion (he will **raise the roof** when he finds out how much this cost)

rays: Narrow beams of light [e.g., **rays** of sunshine; **X-rays**]; a slight showing of anything (there are some **rays** of hope that he might recover); a type of fish with a flat body [e.g., sting**rays**]

raze: To demolish or pull down (we will **raze** these buildings so a new shopping centre can be constructed)

rap/wrap

rap: To strike or knock with a light blow (you will need to **rap** hard on the door, as the occupant is slightly deaf); colloquial: to take the blame (he took the **rap** for the robbery)

wrap: To cover (we always **wrap** our presents on Christmas Eve and place them under the tree); to end a session (let's **wrap** this up now); to keep secret (we will keep this under **wrap** until July 1)

rapped/rapt/wrapped

rapped: Past tense of the verb "to rap" (the young boy was **rapped** on the knuckles for answering back)

rapt: Entranced or enraptured (the students were **rapt** in amazement at the experiment)

wrapped: Past tense of the verb "to wrap" (Paul **wrapped** a blanket around the fire victim)

rapt/wrapped/rapped (see rapped/rapt/wrapped)

ray/re

ray: A narrow beam of light (the **ray** of light from the torch was sufficient to illuminate the path); a small amount of expectation, thought, etc. (the doctor offered a **ray** of hope that the cancer was treatable); in physics, any of the lines or streams in which light appears to flow; in mathematics, one of a system of straight lines appearing from a point; in astronomy, one of the many observed streaks of light coming from the craters of the moon; a new technology, a disc that allows a large amount of storage of high-definition material (Blu-**ray** technology has begun to transform the way we store films); a fish related to sharks that has gill openings (the **ray** usually has a flattened body so that it can lie concealed on the sea floor)

re: In music, part of a scale [e.g., do, **re**, mi, fa, so, la, ti]

rays/raze/raise (see raise/rays/raze)

raze/raise/rays (see raise/rays/raze)

re/ray (see ray/re)

read/red

read: The past tense of the verb "to read" (she **read** a book to her mother who was ill); also used as an adjective (he is a widely **read** person in the field of mathematics)

red: A color (the America flag is **red**, white, and blue); a reference to a negative bank balance (the firm is in the **red**, so we will have to reduce our expenses); colloquial: to be angry or humiliated (all he could do was **see red** when the sports car ran into his sedan)

read/reed

read: To peruse and understand the meaning of a book, etc. (the student had to **read** Shakespeare's *The Tempest* for her literature class); to utter something written (he was asked to **read** the newspaper out loud to his grandfather); to sense an emotion (Sarah was able to **read** his face and knew she had upset him); to tell someone's fortune (her ability to **read** the cards was widely known); colloquial: something that is enjoyable to read (this book is a good **read**); colloquial: to understand (she was able to **read between the lines** and knew he was going to break off the engagement)

reed: A straight stalk of various grasses (**reeds** often grow in marshy areas); a piece of thin cane or metal attached to wind instruments that vibrates to produce a sound (double-**reed** instruments such as the oboe and the English horn are found in most modern orchestras)

real/reel

real: Actual; having existence (a rabbit is **real** but the Tooth Fairy is imaginary); true (the **real** reason he left his job is he wanted an increase in salary); genuine, and not a fake (this is a **real** diamond); colloquial: the genuine article (this clock is the **real McCoy**)

reel: A rotary wheel on which rope, wire, etc. is wound (lifeguards are trained to use a **reel** with rope attached to the lifeguard to rescue surfers in trouble); the round cylinder to wind film or thread on (remember to wind the cotton on the **reel** before you start to use the sewing machine); the act of pulling in fish, etc. (be careful when you **reel** in the snapper) red/read (see read/red)

reed/read (see read/reed)

reek/wreak

reek: To emit vapor, steam, or fumes or to smell offensive (the kitchen will **reek** of garlic if you put that much in the pot)

wreak: To be destructive as a result of rage, anger, alcoholism, etc. (he is known to **wreak** havoc in the household after drinking too much)

reel/real (see real/reel)

reign/rein/rain (see rain/reign/rein)

rein/rain/reign (see rain/reign/rein)

residence/residents

residence: The place where someone lives (his **residence** is located in New York); an impressive house (this is a magnificent **residence**); the fact of residing in a particular place (the cat has taken up **residence** in the lounge room); the time of living in or occupying a place (many students have been **in residence** at the university hall for over three years)

residents: The people who live in a house, occupy a room in a hotel, or occupy an area (the **residents** in this tree-lined suburb are very quiet)

residents/residence (see residence/residents)

rest/wrest

rest: To relax or sleep (many toddlers take an afternoon **rest**); to stop a machine for a short while (I will give the tractor a **rest** before beginning on the next field); colloquial: to cease (just give it a **rest**, because we will never agree); to bury (he has been **laid to rest**); in music, a symbol that indicates an interval where an instrument does not play; the remainder (eat the **rest** of your dinner or you won't go outside to play); all of the others (the **rest** of us are too tired to join you); colloquial: to allow your reputation to rely on past achievements (after a splendid record of spin bowling, he could now **rest on his laurels**)

wrest: To take something from someone by twisting and turning and using force (John said he would **wrest** the knife from Kevin to stop him hurting himself and others if Kevin didn't willingly give up the knife)

retch/wretch

retch: To vomit or make attempts to vomit (Taylor has been trying to **retch** since she ate the grasshopper)

wretch: A person who is in physical, financial, or emotional distress (the poor **wretch** is in so much gambling trouble); someone who is despicable in character (he is a despicable **wretch** who sells drugs to adolescents)

review/revue

review: An evaluation of a book, film, art exhibition, etc. (Alan was very upset with the **review** of his book when it appeared in the newspaper); a journal, magazine, etc. that reviews literature, artworks, finance, and current affairs (the *Australian Financial Review* is a highly respected journal reporting the latest news from business, finance, investments, and politics); to look over something again (we will need to **review** these plans for the new building to ensure that they comply with the current regulations); in law, to re-examine (the judge will **review** the sentence imposed on the prisoner)

revue: A theatrical entertainment in which different performers parody recent events or people in either song or acting (university **revues** are popular and have been a stepping-stone for some famous actors)

revue/review (see review/revue)

rhyme/rime

rhyme: Used mainly in poetry or verse where one word corresponds in sound with another [e.g., shout and pout, hill and spill, usually at the end of a line] (the nursery **rhyme** "Baa, Baa, Black Sheep" has entertained children for many years); a phrase indicating a lack of logic, explanation, meaning (there is no **rhyme** or reason for your decision to ban the performance)

rime: A white icy covering found on trees, etc. formed from fog or mist

rigger/rigor

rigger: A person who makes a ship or yacht ready for sailing (the **rigger** has rigged and checked the sails ready for the race to begin); similarly, someone who readies an airplane for flight

rigor: Exactitude, severity, allowing no latitude (the dean of the faculty commented that although the workload on academics was increasing, academic **rigor** must be maintained)

right/rite/write

right: Correct or appropriate (it is important to use the **right** word when you are writing); the opposite of left (remember to turn **right** at the next corner); to be well (yes, I am all **right** now that I have recovered from the flu); ownership (I have the **right** to this house); legally, a just claim (he has the **right** to have a solicitor); morally, to be good or proper (it is only **right** that the people affected by the floods should receive government help)

rite: A formal ceremony (many churches practice the **rite** of baptism)

write: To form words or characters on paper or similar using a pen or pencil (I need to **write** my name on this form); to communicate in writing (please **write** a letter to the company regarding the faulty merchandise); in computers, to copy information from the hard drive onto a disc

rigor/rigger (see rigger/rigor)

rime/rhyme (see rhyme/rime)

ring/wring

ring: A circular band of metal, usually silver or gold, often set with jewels, worn on the finger for ornamental purposes or as a symbol of marriage, betrothal, etc. (Gillian excitedly showed her friends her diamond engagement **ring**); a circle (the Olympic Games is symbolized by five different colored **rings**); a round circular area (at agricultural shows, cattle are paraded around the **ring**); a group of people (he is a member of a drug **ring**); to encircle (the children formed a **ring** around the teacher); to make a resonant sound (the church bells **ring** early every Sunday morning); colloquial: to compete (to throw one's hat in the **ring**)

wring: To press, squeeze, or twist (remember to **wring** the water out of the clothes before you hang them outside to dry); colloquial: to be annoyed (I could **wring your neck** for hitting your brother)

rite/write/right (see right/rite/write)

road/rode/rowed

road: A way used by people, cars, bicycles, etc. (cars often have to wait until the farmer moves his cows across the **road**); colloquial: to begin a journey (I must **hit the road** or I won't get there before night); colloquial: to have a last drink (have **one for the road** before you leave)

rode: Past tense of the verb "to ride" (he **rode** his bicycle to school)

rowed: Past tense of the verb "to row," meaning to use oars to propel a boat on water (she **rowed** in the school's rowing championships)

roam/Rome

roam: To walk, wander, or ramble (he is known to **roam** for hours through the countryside)

Rome: The capital city of Italy (I visited many ancient ruins as well as the Colosseum in **Rome** when I toured Europe)

rode/rowed/road (see road/rode/rowed)

role/roll

role: The part or character an actor plays in the theatre or a film (her **role** as Cleopatra in *Antony and Cleopatra* was acclaimed by the critics); a certain position or function (he hated his **role** as the disciplinarian in the family)

roll: To move along a surface by turning over and over (the ball would often **roll** down the driveway); to move on wheels (Jack, **roll** the wagon closer to the shed); to spread out (for the Academy Awards they **roll** out the red carpet for the celebrities to walk on); to move from side to side (a ship's **roll** can make you seasick); the sound of thunder (the dogs get upset when they hear the **roll** of thunder); also a form of bread or pastry (will you have a **roll** or just a slice of bread?); colloquial: to prepare to work hard (he often would **roll up his sleeves** to pitch in and help)

roll/role (see role/roll)

Rome/roam (see roam/Rome)

root/route

> **root:** The part of a tree or plant that is below the surface of the ground and is divided into tendrils that absorb moisture and nutriments (be careful of the **root** system when you are digging so you don't kill the plant); the fundamental part or the source (the **root** of the matter is that you need to study if you want to do well on your exams); colloquial: to find (could you **root** around the office and find my notes?); to support (I always **root for** the underdogs)

> **route:** The way taken when traveling (the **route** we took when we sailed to Britain was via the Suez Canal and along the Mediterranean)

rose/rows

> **rose:** One of the most loved flowers with a variety of colors and prickly stems (a red **rose** is appreciated by most females, particularly on Valentine's Day); a beautiful female (she is a **rose** among the thorns); the past tense of the verb "to rise" (he **rose** from his chair to greet his guests)

> **rows:** Rowing a boat (he **rows** well); seats in lines in theatres, sporting arenas, etc. (make certain you get a seat in the first few **rows** or you miss a lot of the action)

rote/wrote

> **rote:** To do something in a mechanical manner without thought (I am so used to driving my car to work that I do it **by rote**)

wrote: Past tense of "to write" (he **wrote** a letter home to his mother every week)

route/root (see root/route)

rowed/road/rode (see road/rode/rowed)

rows/rose (see rose/rows)

rung/wrung

rung: Past tense of the verb "to ring" (the school bell was always **rung** at 9 a.m. and 3 p.m.); each step of a ladder (she very carefully puts one foot at a time on each **rung** as she climbs the ladder); a stage in progress (the next **rung** will be passing her university exams and gaining her bachelor of arts degree)

wrung: Past participle of the verb "to wring," meaning to twist or squeeze to remove water (before automatic washing machines it was common practice for clothes to be **wrung** before being hung on a clothesline to dry); colloquial: to be annoyed (I could have **wrung his neck** when he came home with dirty boots and muddied the floor I had just washed)

rye/wry

rye: A type of grain used in cereals, bread, and a type of whiskey (American whiskey can be divided into three main categories: bourbon, Tennessee, and **rye**)

wry: A facial expression indicating dislike or discomfort (she responded with a **wry** smile when he suggested a picnic lunch to celebrate her birthday)

≥ S ≤

sac/sack

sac: A biological term, referring to a bag-like structure containing fluid found in humans and animals (the amniotic **sac** containing water plays an important role in the development of the fetus in the uterus)

sack: A large bag made of coarse material used for storing or transporting goods such as grain and potatoes (before the days of air conditioners, central heating, or solar panels, a **sack** of coal would be delivered to households for heating purposes); colloquial: the pillaging and destruction of defeated cities, etc. by victorious armies (the **sack** of Rome by the armies of the Holy Roman emperor Charles V, in 1527, ended the city's dominance in the Renaissance); colloquial: a bed (he was so tired, he **hit the sack**)

sachet/sashay

sachet: A small sealed bag used to contain goods such as perfumed powder, cosmetics, or food (it was customary for women to place a perfumed **sachet** among their lingerie)

sashay: To move extravagantly; to flounce (she was known to **sashay** among her guests to attract attention)

sack/sac (see sac/sack)

sail/sale

sail: The expanse of canvas on a boat used to capture the wind to move the vessel through the water (the ships of yesterday were fitted with **sails** but today they are used mainly on recreational crafts); to travel through water (it is a beautiful sight to see the yachts **sail** out of the harbor); to set out on a voyage (we will set **sail** for the Bahamas); the arm of a windmill

sale: The act of selling goods (supermarkets are renowned for the variety of goods they have for **sale**); also refers to goods reduced in price at the end of a season or after special occasions (the **sale** after Christmas attracts large numbers of customers looking for bargains)

sale/sail (see sail/sale)

sashay/sachet (see sachet/sashay)

scene/seen

scene: A division of a play (I think **scene** 1 in act 2 was the best part of the play); a view (snow on top of the mountains is a beautiful **scene**); a place of interest or a situation (the police asked us to leave the **scene** of the accident); the atmosphere of a specific activity or interest (the pop **scene** attracts those aged from 11 to the late teens); to display bad temper (please don't **make a scene** in front of our guests)

seen: Past tense of the verb "to see," meaning to observe or to be observed (I have **seen** that happen before)

scent/sent/cent (see cent/scent/sent)

scents/sense/cents (see cents/scents/sense)

scull/skull

scull: One of a set of small oars used by a single rower on a light racing boat (he broke the **scull** just before reaching the finishing line and lost the race); also an oar across the stern, worked with twisting strokes to propel a boat

skull: The bony framework of the head that encloses the brain (an injury to the **skull** is extremely serious); part of a pirate's ensign (the **skull**-and-crossbones flag brought shudders to many sailors)

sea/see/C (see C/sea/see)

sealing/ceiling (see ceiling/sealing)

seam/seem

seam: A line formed when two pieces of cloth, etc. are sewn together (Betsy, you will have to undo that **seam**, because it is not straight); in geology, a thin layer or stratum usually between two larger strata (the miners picked at the **seam** of coal in the underground)

seem: Appear to be (you always **seem** so happy and carefree); to appear to yourself (I always **seem** to be the one washing the dishes); to be apparent (it would **seem** most likely that the firm will not make a profit this year)

sear/seer

sear: To burn the surface of or to scorch (be careful with the iron so you don't **sear** your shirt); to dry up or wither (the oppressive heat will **sear** the crops)

seer: A prophet; one who foretells what will happen in the future

seas/sees/seize

seas: Plural of "sea" (a common expression is "to sail the seven **seas**")

sees: Plural of "to see" (my father always **sees** everything we do that is wrong)

seize: To grab hold of (I will **seize** this gun from you before you do any harm); to take by force (the plan is to **seize** the ammunition fort held by the enemy); to take possession by legal means or to confiscate (the police under law can search and **seize** illegal drugs); to become stuck or jammed through heat, etc. (the engine will **seize up** if you don't keep water and oil at the recommended level)

see/C/sea (see C/sea/see)

seed/cede (see cede/seed)

seem/seam (see seam/seem)

seen/scene (see scene/seen)

seer/sear (see sear/seer)

sees/seize/seas (see seas/sees/seize)

seize/seas/sees (see seas/sees/seize)

sell/cell (see cell/sell)

seller/cellar (see cellar/seller)

sense/cents/scents (see cents/scents/sense)

sensor/censer/censor (see censer/censor/sensor)

sent/cent/scent (see cent/scent/sent)

serf/surf

> **serf:** A farm laborer forced to work for his landowning lord in the Middle Ages (many a wife today complains she is treated as a **serf**)

> **surf:** The waves of the sea as they break on the shore (swimmers are warned not to enter the water if the **surf** is rough); to ride a wave toward the shore with your body or a board (if you are going to **surf**, make sure you stay between the flags in the ocean)

serge/surge

> **serge:** A strong twilled fabric used to make clothing (our winter school uniforms were always made of **serge** material)

> **surge:** A strong movement either upward or forward (the **surge** of the waves kept the surfers out of the water); a wave-like rush of emotion (he had a **surge** of exhilaration when competing in the race); in mechanics, the unevenness in an engine (he was aware of the intermittent **surge** in the engine and thought he should stop)

serial/cereal (see cereal/serial)

session/cession (see cession/session)

sew/so/sow

> **sew:** To stitch pieces of cloth or similar together with a needle and thread or a sewing machine (girls were taught to **sew** by their mothers or at school in the 20th century)
>
> **so:** To do in a way indicated (you should do it just **so**); to a certain degree (you should not talk **so** fast, as no one can understand you); to emphasize (I am **so** tired); continuing in the same way, similar to etcetera (and **so** on and **so** forth); in music, part of a scale [e.g., do, re, mi, fa, **so**, la, ti]
>
> **sow:** To scatter seed over the ground (in spring, farmers **sow** their fields)

shear/sheer

> **shear:** To cut with a sharp instrument (tailors **shear** material to make suits); to remove or deprive (the government has threatened to **shear** money from the budget previously available for school improvements)
>
> **sheer:** Transparently thin material (the material in her dress was so **sheer** that you could see her underwear); complete or unqualified (it was a **sheer** waste of time and money to build a new courthouse); extending up or down very sharply (I don't know if I will be able to climb this **sheer** rock); to deviate from a course (the car was able to **sheer** to the left to avoid the cattle on the road)

sheer/shear (see shear/sheer)

shoe/shoo

shoe: Footwear, usually of leather or canvas, with a softer upper and a heavier sole (when Marion opened the box, she found she had one **shoe** a larger size than the other); also a horseshoe used to protect a horse's feet (the horse**shoe** is kept often to bring luck or good fortune); a piece of metal used to activate the brake drum of a car

shoo: An expression used to scatter animals or birds (the boys always **shoo** the bees away when they come too close); colloquial: a likely winner (he will be a **shoo-in** at the next election)

shoo/shoe (see shoe/shoo)

shoot/chute (see chute/shoot)

sic/sick

sic: A word entered after an incorrect word to indicate that the statement is being quoted as written or spoken ("we have decided not to procede [**sic**] with the building of a new bridge..."); to incite a dog to attack (move away or I will **sic** my dog on you)

sick: To be unwell or ill (I was so **sick** with the flu I had to stay in bed for three days); to be affected by emotion (when I saw on the news that there were children killed in the accident, I felt **sick** at heart); disgusting (that photo is really **sick**); to be fed up with something (I am **sick and tired** of all your complaints); colloquial: something great or terrific (this car is **sick**)

sick/sic (see sic/sick)

side/sighed

> **side:** The position to the right or left of an object or place (the wound is on the right **side** of the left leg); surfaces of an object (I like to print my photos on the shiny **side** of the paper); to support another in argument (Liz is on her brother's **side** regarding the treatment of refugees); a line of descent (the color of her eyes came from her mother's **side** of the family); to leave for later consideration (I will put writing this to the **side** until I have finished reading the newspaper)

> **sighed:** Past tense of "to sigh," meaning to let out breath slowly, indicating tiredness, relief, or sorrow (Margaret **sighed** in relief when she was told her son had been found)

sighed/side (see side/sighed)

sighs/size

> **sighs:** Plural of "sigh," meaning a slow exhalation of breath (the **sighs** of relief from the audience could be heard when the trapeze artist successfully caught the rope)

> **size:** The dimensions or magnitude of an object (you will never be able to eat a steak that **size**); one of a series of graduated measurements (my shoe **size** is 8 but my daughter wears a **size** 10); colloquial: to form an estimate of someone (it was easy to **size her up** and know she was only after his money)

sight/site/cite (see cite/sight/site)

sign/sine

> **sign:** An indication (the teacher gave a **sign** for the children to stop talking); a conventional figure used instead of words (the flashing lights were a **sign** for drivers to slow down); an inscribed board (the "for sale" **sign** on the house attracted a few would-be purchasers); to affix a signature (please **sign** on the dotted line); to recruit new players (the rugby league team decided to **sign** on two new forwards); to finish (I will **sign off** now, thanks for listening); language for the deaf (**sign** language on television programs has been beneficial for many deaf people)
>
> **sine:** A mathematical trigonometric measure

signet/cygnet (see cygnet/signet)

sine/sign (see sign/sine)

sink/sync

> **sink:** To fall gradually into the ground (this chair will **sink** if you put it on that soggy ground); to fall gradually into the sea or ocean (unless you take some of the passengers off the boat, it will **sink**); a receptacle to wash dishes in (the **sink** is full of dirty dishes); to fall lower in estimation or rank (you will **sink** in her estimation if you wear those clothes); colloquial: to have the two options of failure or success (in my opinion, you should let her **sink or swim**)
>
> **sync:** Shortened form of "synchronization"; in time with (her feet tapped **in sync** with the music)

Sioux/sue

Sioux: A Native American tribe (the **Sioux** were discovered by the French in 1640, near the headwaters of the Mississippi River)

sue: To institute an action in law against someone (the landlord intends to **sue** him for not paying his rent); also a common female name (**Sue** is a shortened form of "Susan")

site/cite/sight (see cite/sight/site)

size/sighs (see sighs/size)

skull/scull (see scull/skull)

slay/sleigh

slay: To kill (please don't **slay** all the animals); colloquial: to impress (you should see him in concert because he will **slay** you)

sleigh: A sledge on runners used for carrying people or goods and normally pulled by dogs or horses (Santa Claus is usually pictured on Christmas cards arriving in a **sleigh** pulled by reindeer)

sleigh/slay (see slay/sleigh)

sleight/slight

sleight: Dexterity and cunning used to deceive (with **sleight of hand**, the magician made the coin disappear)

slight: A small amount or degree (there was only a **slight** increase in inflation this year); of little importance (it was only a **slight** lapse, and it won't happen again); slender or slim (she is so **slight** that she only wears a size 4); an insult (that remark was definitely a **slight**)

slight/sleight (see sleight/slight)

so/sow/sew (see sew/so/sow)

soar/sore

soar: To fly upward (we stopped to watch the bird **soar** into the sky); in aeronautics, to fly without engine power (it was a beautiful sight to see the glider **soar** over the water); to rise higher (this student will **soar** to great heights; economists fear the dollar will **soar** further)

sore: A wound (he has a **sore** on his leg); feeling pain (Bill felt **sore** all over after falling from a horse); colloquial: to be visibly different from the rest (she stuck out **like a sore thumb**)

soared/sword

soared: Past tense of "to soar," meaning to fly upward (the birds **soared** into the air when they were disturbed); rose in emotion (her spirits **soared** when she heard she had passed her exams)

sword: A weapon typically long with either a straight or curved sharp pointed blade used in the Middle Ages through to World War II to kill the enemy (the **sword** today is used more for ceremonial purposes such as the Queen's investiture (knighting) ceremony in Great Britain)

sold/soled

sold: Past tense of "to sell," meaning to dispose of goods to someone for payment (I **sold** the old vinyl records on eBay for $100); to convince someone (I **sold** him on the idea); colloquial: to be enthusiastic (she was **sold** on the idea of going overseas for 12 months); colloquial: to sell very quickly, usually in large quantities (the clothes at a reduced price **sold like hot cakes**)

soled: Put a new sole on a shoe, boot, etc. (the repairer said the shoes were too damaged to be **soled**)

sole/soul

sole: The only one (this is the **sole** carving knife left in the shop); belonging exclusively to a person or a group (he has the **sole** right to ownership of the farm); also the undersurface of a foot or shoe, sandal, etc. (when I stood on a stone, I hurt the **sole** of my foot); a type of flatfish with a hook-like snout (the children were excited when they caught a **sole**)

soul: Believed to be the spiritual part of a human being distinct from the physical being (in Christian theology, the **soul** is considered to be immortal); metaphorically, to affect one's emotions or senses (this music touches my **soul**); a description of a person with a kind nature (she is a kind **soul**)

soled/sold (see sold/soled)

some/sum

some: An unspecified person, thing, or quantity (**some** scoundrel threw a stone through the window); an unspecified but fairly large amount or size (that baby is **some** size; you have had my book for **some** time); an approximate amount (**some** of us will come to help you build your garage); colloquial: great or important (that was **some** compliment the boss gave you)

sum: To total by adding, subtracting, etc. (what is the **sum** of 6 × 3 + 25?); an unspecified quantity (I can only lend you a small **sum**); the total amount (the **sum** of money owing comes to $26); to review a discussion or viewpoint (finally, to **sum up** what we have discussed); to make a quick estimate (it is easy to **sum up** what he is thinking)

son/sun

son: Male offspring of his parents (Peter is the second **son** of Nancy and Don); an expression used paternally to a young male (**son**, come over here and see the ships coming into the harbor)

sun: A star around which the earth revolves and which gives light and energy (the **sun** goes down in the night and rises in the morning); colloquial: in the world, on earth (he is the most ignorant person **under the sun**)

sore/soar (see soar/sore)

soul/sole (see sole/soul)

sow/sew/so (see sew/so/sow)

spade/spayed

spade: An implement for digging (I can't dig with this broken **spade**); one of the suits in a pack of cards (you need a **spade**, not a heart); colloquial: to call it as it is (let's call **a spade a spade**)

spayed: Past tense of "to spay," meaning to remove the ovaries of a female animal (we had our two female dogs **spayed** after they had litters)

spayed/spade (see spade/spayed)

spec/speck

spec: A detailed description of work to be done (I will have the **spec** for the new building by the end of the week); a hope or aspiration (I have bought these shares on **spec** and am hoping they will rise over the next few months)

speck: A small spot often a different color from its background (there is a **speck** of blue paint on your jacket); a fragment of dust, soot, etc. (I think I have a **speck** of dust in my eye); away in the distance (that car passed us so quickly, it is now only a **speck** on the horizon)

speck/spec (see spec/speck)

staid/stayed

staid: Sedate or settled (she is a very **staid** woman, not adventurous or flighty)

stayed: Past tense of "to stay" (she **stayed** up late to watch the end of the baseball game)

stair/stare

stair: One of a series in a flight of steps leading upward (mind that **stair** when you climb up, as it is very unsteady)

stare: To look fixedly (don't take any notice when they **stare** at you); to gaze at something without really seeing it (he gave me such a glassy **stare** that it was unnerving); to look at someone without blinking

stake/steak

stake: A stick or post pointed at one end used as part of a fence or a boundary marking (Ken used a mallet to drive the **stake** into the ground to mark where the fence was to go); a post used in executions, particularly for burnings in the Middle Ages (Joan of Arc, the Maid of Orléans, was burned at the **stake** in 1431); a support for plants and to tether animals; to assert your claim (to **stake out** a gold-mining claim); colloquial: a wager in a game, contest, etc. or the funds a gambler uses (I will **stake** $50 to your $10 that I can beat you in a 100-yard dash); to give funds in return for later reward (he decided to take a **stake** in the fledgling company as he believed it would eventually be successful)

steak: A slice of meat, usually beef, ham, or fish (Ron likes his T-bone **steak** grilled medium rare and with pepper sauce and vegetables)

stare/stair (see stair/stare)

stationary/stationery

stationary: Standing still, not moving (the crowd was **stationary**, waiting for the doors to the theater to open)

stationery: Writing paper, envelopes, pens, pencils, etc. (we are low on **stationery**, particularly paper clips and envelopes, so we need to stop at the office supply store)

stationery/stationary (see stationary/stationery)

stayed/staid (see staid/stayed)

steak/stake (see stake/steak)

steal/steel

steal: To take goods dishonestly, without permission (young kids used to **steal** lollipops from shops); to take someone else's ideas (in business, it is not unusual for industrial spies to **steal** new ideas or plans); to leave a place unobtrusively (Jim would often **steal away** from the meeting when no one was looking); colloquial: to outshine (Alex is known to **steal the show** when he appears in a play); colloquial: something obtained cheaply (it was a **steal**)

steel: An artificially produced form of iron (**steel** can be used for varied purposes such as building frameworks, gates, tools, etc.); to stiffen (she had to **steel** herself, fearing the worst after her daughter's accident)

steel/steal (see steal/steel)

stile/style

stile: An arrangement of steps that allows a person to ascend or descend over a fence, etc. that is enclosing a field (if a horse charges you, you will need to get over that **stile** quickly)

style: A particular way of doing things in writing, dress, acting, playing sport, etc. (her writing **style** is similar to that of Agatha Christie); a way of living (as a couple, they live in a very simple **style**)

straight/strait

straight: Not curved or bent (the teacher told the student to draw a **straight** line down the page); a "hand" in cards (a **straight** in poker is five cards of various suits in sequence); a description of someone who is direct in his dealings (Simon is totally **straight** and will tell you if your car is worth repairing); an undiluted drink (I will have a **straight** whiskey, with no mixers); colloquial: a heterosexual person (he is **straight**, not gay); colloquial: to stay out of trouble and obey the law (Laura intends to stay **straight** now that she is out of prison)

strait: A narrow stretch of water connecting two seas (the Magellan **Strait** is an important natural passage between the Pacific and the Atlantic oceans); in plural form also means being in financial or social difficulty (poor Frank is in **dire straits**, having lost his wife, his house, and his job)

strait/straight (see straight/strait)

style/stile (see stile/style)

sue/Sioux (see Sioux/sue)

suede/swayed

> **suede:** Leather with the flesh side rubbed to achieve a soft, velvety touch, used for handbags, jackets, gloves, etc. (**suede** gloves are not as popular today as they were years ago)

> **swayed:** Past tense of "to sway," meaning to move from side to side (the mother **swayed** when she heard the news of her child's accident); changed someone's opinion (the speech against racism was so compelling that it **swayed** the crowd that had gathered to listen)

suite/sweet

> **suite:** A number of rooms connected in a hotel, etc. (it is quite common for honeymooners to book the bridal **suite** in an upscale hotel); a lounge and two armchairs (the leather lounge **suite** was one of the first purchases we made when we moved to our new home); a musical work [e.g., the Cinderella **Suite**, seven descriptive pieces for pianoforte by composer Frank Hutchens]

> **sweet:** A taste or food that is the opposite of sour, usually containing sugar, such as cakes, chocolate, etc. (this chocolate is smooth and **sweet**); a strong liking for sweets (he is known to have **a sweet tooth**); a pleasant sound (the **sweet** sound of birds chirping); a person who is amiable or kind (she is such a **sweet** person who is always smiling and helpful)

sum/some (see some/sum)

summary/summery

> **summary:** A brief and comprehensive statement
> or document that sums up the relevant points (the
> **summary** at the end of the paper covers all the major
> points)

> **summery:** Having the qualities of summer (even
> though it is still only spring, it is quite **summery** today)

summery/summary (see summary/summery)

sun/son (see son/sun)

surf/serf (see serf/surf)

surge/serge (see serge/surge)

swayed/suede (see suede/swayed)

sweet/suite (see suite/sweet)

sword/soared (see soared/sword)

symbol/cymbal (see cymbal/symbol)

sync/sink (see sink/sync)

⋛ T ⋚

T/tea/tee/ti

> **T:** The 20th letter in the alphabet; a crosspiece, as in a
> T-square, T-intersection, or three-way joint pipe fitting

(the **T**-intersection and **T**-square are so named because both the intersection and the measuring instrument resemble a letter **T**)

tea: The dried and prepared leaves of a shrub that when infused in water become one of the most popular drinks in the world (**tea** is cultivated mainly in India, Sri Lanka, and China, and can be served either hot or iced, and with or without milk or sugar); colloquial: rejecting an idea or request (I wouldn't go on the stage and sing **for all the tea in China**); something that is in keeping with your liking (talking to students is much more my **cup of tea**)

tee: The starting place to hit off in golf from each fairway (the house overlooked the fifth **tee** of a golf course); a small wooden object or mound of dirt on which the ball is placed (it was not unusual to see the **tee** fly up into the air when the golf ball was mis-hit); colloquial: when a garment suits or fits someone very well (that black dress suits you **to a tee**)

ti: In music, part of a scale [e.g., do, re, mi, fa, so, la, **ti**]

tacks/tax

tacks: Small, sharp-pointed pins or nails with flat heads (boys and girls use **tacks** to pin up posters in their rooms); long stitches used to join two seams together before sewing by machine (don't forgot to take all those **tacks** out after you have sewn your dress); a nautical term referring to the direction or course of a vessel in relation to the position of its sails (she is very proficient in the way she **tacks** to take advantage of the wind)

tax: The amount paid to the government based on the salary earned (if I get a raise, I will move into the next **tax** bracket); the amount the government receives from land and property sales, goods purchased, companies' profits, etc.; to put pressure or a burden on (cryptic crosswords certainly **tax** my brain)

tail/tale

tail: The appendage that hangs from an animal's rear (Rani, our dog, wags her **tail** in excitement when she sees the leash and hears the word "walk"); the rear of a march, parade, etc. (Shirley found herself at the **tail** end of the march with the other stragglers); the reverse side of a coin (when the umpire tosses the coin to see who will serve first in a tennis match, the call is made "heads" or "**tails**"); in formal attire for men, refers to the skirt on a formal coat (men always look more attractive in **tails**); to follow someone (the private detective was told to **tail** his client's husband); colloquial: to be busy, trying to catch up on jobs (Jonathan is always **chasing his tail**); colloquial: to be humiliated (he left **with his tail between his legs**)

tale: A story, either factual or fiction, spoken or written (*A **Tale** of Two Cities,* a book about the French Revolution, was written by Charles Dickens in 1859); a lie or falsehood (Mom could always tell if I was telling her a **tale**)

tale/tail (see tail/tale)

tare/tear

tare: The allowance made for the weight of the container in which goods are packed or the weight of a vehicle when it is empty (many trucks have the **tare** weight indicated on the side of the vehicle)

tear: To rip or split apart (would you please **tear** the section out of the newspaper that lists movie times for tonight?); the result of someone pulling hard (I have a **tear** in my shirt because you pulled it so hard); colloquial: to demolish (it's sad to see them **tear down** that beautiful old house)

taught/taut

taught: Past tense of "to teach," meaning to impart knowledge or give instruction (Mr. Stephens **taught** history at our school)

taut: Tense or tightly drawn (her face was **taut** with worry about whether her family survived the earthquake)

taut/taught (see taught/taut)

tax/tacks (see tacks/tax)

tea/tee/ti/T (see T/tea/tee/ti)

team/teem

team: A number of persons or animals involved in a joint activity (the hockey **team** was cheered by thousands when they won the Stanley Cup); to work together (we must work as a **team** if we expect to complete this task on time)

teem: A large quantity (move that brick and you will see a **teem** of ants)

tear/tare (see tare/tear)

tear/tier

tear: A drop of liquid falling from the eye usually caused by grief, pain, emotion, etc. (a **tear** rolled down her cheek when she saw the television news broadcast of the human suffering in Africa)

tier: A series of rows leading upward (your seat is in the second **tier**)

teas/tease/tees

teas: Plural of "tea" (how many **teas** and coffees are available?)

tease: To annoy or irritate by petty remarks or requests or to make fun of someone (why do you take her toys and **tease** your sister all the time?); to comb hair to give it body and increase its height (Jenny finds it difficult to **tease** her hair when it has been cut too short); a flirt (she is such a **tease** the way she tosses her hair and smiles at all the boys)

tees: The third person singular of "tee" (he **tees** off and watches until his ball lands, hopefully much further along the fairway); plural of "tee" (I keep extra **tees** in my pocket when playing golf)

tease/teas/tees (see teas/tease/tees)

tee/ti/T/tea (see T/tea/tee/ti)

teem/team (see team/teem)

tees/teas/tease (see teas/tease/tees)

tense/tents

>**tense:** Tightly drawn, rigid, taut (he pulled the wire **tense** to ensure that no cattle could get through the fence); in a strained mental state (Pat was **tense** waiting for the results of the biopsy of the lump in her breast); an adjective describing the strain on feelings (it was a **tense** time waiting for the exam results); in grammar, the category of a verb (a verb can be in the future, present, or past **tense**)
>
>**tents:** Portable canvas shelters (many groups such as the Boy Scouts and Girl Guides as well as families use **tents** when camping)

tents/tense (see tense/tents)

tern/turn

>**tern:** A type of seabird with long pointed wings and a forked tail (the **tern** is similar to the gull but is smaller and more graceful)
>
>**turn:** To rotate or move to the right or left (**turn** the hot tap on the left for the water to come out); to direct movement (you need to **turn** onto Maitland Road and then continue on); to change color (the leaves **turn** brown in the winter)

Thai/tie

Thai: A person born in Thailand; a description of food that is typical of Thailand (we often dine out at **Thai** restaurants, as we particularly enjoy **Thai** food)

tie: To bind together (you need to **tie** the ribbon tightly around the package); a narrow piece of cloth tied around a person's neck (his **tie** is so unfashionable); to restrain (I had to **tie** up the dog so he wouldn't jump over the fence and run away); to have the same score in a sporting event (the game ended in a **tie**); metaphorical: to marry (they are to **tie the knot** in church next Saturday)

their/there/they're

their: The possessive form of the noun "they," meaning belonging to a particular group (it is **their** right to vote for whatever party they want)

there: Indication of a place (the others are standing over **there** waiting for you); to call attention to or to emphasize (hey, you **there**, what do you think you are doing?); colloquial: derogatory term meaning not of sound mind (don't take any notice of her, as she's not **all there**); colloquial: in defiance (if I want to, I will go, **so there**)

they're: A contraction of "they are" (**they're** not quite ready yet, so we'll have to wait)

there/they're/their (see their/there/they're)

they're/their/there (see their/there/they're)

threw/through

threw: Past tense of "to throw," meaning to project (Harry **threw** the stone at the cat but missed and hit the window); to illegally stop or lose a fight (there was uproar from the crowd when the boxer **threw** the fight); colloquial: to put in prison (the police **threw** the men into a cell to sober up)

through: From one end to another and out the other side (the children passed **through** the maze at Hampton Court and came out quickly); to have finished (I finally got **through** all my homework for the week); colloquial: to successfully recover (the doctors have said he will pull **through**); colloquial: the whole extent (those claims of theft were examined **through and through** and were found to be false)

throes/throws

throes: Spasms of emotion or pain (Helen is in the **throes** of childbirth)

throws: Projects (be careful when he **throws** that ball so it doesn't hit you)

throne/thrown

throne: The chair or seat used for ceremonial purposes by kings, queens, the Pope, bishops, etc. (though a **throne** is usually used by reigning monarchs and other dignitaries, a beauty queen can also sit on a **throne** after being crowned)

thrown: A past participle, similar to "threw," meaning projected (the ball was **thrown** by the keeper back to the forward; the case was **thrown** out of court) through/threw (see threw/through)

thrown/throne (see throne/thrown)

throws/throes (see throes/throws)

thyme/time

thyme: A plant that has fragrant, aromatic leaves (**thyme** is used as an herb in cooking to season food)

time: A system of measuring the passage of time (do you realize how much **time** I have wasted waiting for you?); referring to the past or a particular period (the French Revolution was a **time** of upheaval and bloodshed); reference to a particular experience (I hope you have a good **time** tonight at the party; he has had a very hard **time** since he lost his job); to be under pressure (I am working **against time** to complete this essay)

ti/T/tea/tee (see T/tea/tee/ti)

tic/tick

tic: An affliction that causes spasmodic twitching, particularly in the facial muscles and extremities (it is quite difficult to go to interviews for jobs when you are very conscious of having a **tic** that makes your leg contract and move every few minutes)

tick: The beat of a clock, timer, etc. (each **tick** of the clock in the hall tells me to hurry or I will be late for class); a blood-sucking mite (the former tenant told me that it was not unusual to find a **tick** in the bedding) tick/tic (see tic/tick)

tide/tied

>   **tide:** The periodic rise and fall of waters in the ocean
>   owing to the effects of the sun and the moon (don't go
>   swimming in the ocean when it is high **tide**); anything
>   that rises and falls (the **tide** of consumer confidence
>   has waned); colloquial: to oppose (he is going **against
>   the tide** of public opinion); colloquial: to help someone
>   in the short term (I gave him some money to **tide** him
>   over until he received his paycheck)

>   **tied:** Past participle of the verb "to tie," meaning to
>   bind or fasten (that poor horse has been **tied** up all day
>   without any food or water); even scores in a game or
>   sporting event (the rugby league game was **tied** at 24
>   points each); colloquial: to be involved in something
>   else (I am too **tied up** with work to help you with your
>   homework); colloquial: to be married (we **tied the knot**
>   last Saturday)

tie/Thai (see Thai/tie)

tied/tide (see tide/tied)

tier/tear (see tear/tier)

tighten/titan

>   **tighten:** To draw tight (I need to **tighten** the screw on
>   this shelf); to make taut (if you don't stop struggling, I
>   will **tighten** this knot even more); colloquial: to spend
>   less (we need to **tighten our belts** and save our money)

titan: A person or machine that has strength and importance (Rupert Murdoch is a **titan** in the field of newspapers and television)

time/thyme (see thyme/time)

titan/tighten (see tighten/titan)

to/too/two

to: A preposition that is used in multiple ways; to act on (we need **to** go **to** the store **to** buy some groceries); to have an effect on (what will losing your job do **to** your life?); purpose (this train is going **to** Sydney); movement backward and forward, or side to side (he moved **to and fro** waiting for the train to come)

too: Also or in addition to (are you coming to the movies tonight, **too**?); excessive (I have a stomachache because I ate **too** much pie)

two: A cardinal number as the symbol 2; depictions of this number of items or persons (could I please have **two** potatoes with my dinner?; there are **two** of us coming to the party)

toad/towed

toad: A tailless amphibian similar to a frog (the most famous fictional **toad** is "**Mr. Toad**," a character in Kenneth Grahame's book *The Wind in the Willows*); a derogatory term (he is just an ugly, selfish **toad**)

towed: Past tense of the verb "to tow," meaning to pull something behind a car, caravan, etc. (we needed our car **towed** to the garage when it broke down)

toe/tow

toe: One of the digits of the foot (a gorilla's **toe** is used in a similar way to a human's); a part of a stocking or a shoe (the **toe** of his shoe is badly scuffed from kicking stones on the road); colloquial: to conform (Mary is certain to **toe the line** on this proposal)

tow: To drag or pull something along using chains, rope, etc. (Jim decided to **tow** his boat to the campsite so they could go fishing in the lake)

told/tolled

told: Past tense of the verb "to tell," meaning to narrate, inform, etc. (he was upset when he was **told** that his parents were separating); colloquial: to inform on (Abigail **told on** her classmates to the teacher)

tolled: Past tense of the verb "to toll," meaning to sound a bell with slow and regular strokes (the church bell **tolled** every Sunday morning at 8 a.m.)

tolled/told (see told/tolled)

ton/tun

ton: A measurement of weight equal to 2,000 pounds in the United States; colloquial: a heavy weight (when I lifted her, she seemed to **weigh a ton**)

tun: A large cask or barrel used for holding liquids, especially wine, ale, or beer, equal to approximately 252 gallons of wine (you would be very, very drunk if you attempted to drink a **tun** of wine!)

too/two/to (see to/too/two)

tort/torte

tort: A wrongful act, not including a breach of contract, that results in injury to another's person, property, reputation, etc. and for which the injured party is entitled to compensation (writing "pedophile" on the window of someone's house is an example of a **tort**)

torte: A highly decorated rich cake containing cream, etc. (my grandmother made a **torte** with hazelnut, chocolate, and cream for special occasions)

torte/tort (see tort/torte)

tow/toe (see toe/tow)

towed/toad (see toad/towed)

tracked/tract

tracked: Past tense of "to track," meaning to follow or hunt (after information from his informant, the detective **tracked** the suspect to the site of the robbery)

tract: A large stretch of land (he has decided to buy the **tract** of farming land that is up for sale); in anatomy, a system of related parts in the body (the doctor explained that I had a blockage in my digestive **tract**)

tract/tracked (see tracked/tract)

troop/troupe

troop: An assembly or group of people or animals (many children joined either a Girl Scout or Boy Scout **troop**); in the military, a body of soldiers or marines

(they lost many of the men in the **troop** after a tour of duty in Afghanistan)

troupe: A company or band of actors, musicians, or dancers (the traveling **troupe** gave a stunning performance of Shakespeare's A *Midsummer Night's Dream* to a packed audience)

troupe/troop (see troop/troupe)

trussed/trust

trussed: Tied up or fastened (the kidnappers had him **trussed** up with ropes around his feet and hands)

trust: To rely on the integrity of others (I **trust** our accountant to handle all our finances); confidence in someone paying later for goods (the shop owner gave him the goods **on trust**, confident he would pay the amount by the end of the week); to leave goods, etc. in someone's care (I left my briefcase **in the trust** of my secretary while I was out at lunch)

trust/trussed (see trussed/trust)

tun/ton (see ton/tun)

turn/tern (see tern/turn)

two/to/too (see to/too/two)

꒰ U ꒱

urn/earn (see earn/urn)

use/yews/ewes (see ewes/use/yews)

⋛ V ⋚

vain/vane/vein

vain: Having excessive pride in one's appearance, achievements, etc. (he is so **vain** that he is always looking at himself in the mirror); futile and without effect (she looked **in vain** for him in the crowd); blasphemous (to take God's name **in vain**)

vane: A flat piece of metal or wood erected in a high position that reacts to the wind and shows which way it is blowing (many people have a weather**vane** that resembles a rooster in their garden)

vein: One of a system of vessels that conveys blood to the heart (Marion had a blocked **vein** and needed medical attention); one of the strands of vascular tissue running through a leaf (if you hold the leaf to the light, you can see each **vein**)

vale/veil

vale: Land between two hills often with a stream coursing through; a valley; a dale (today, the word "**vale**" is used more in a poetic sense)

veil: A piece of light, transparent material used to cover the face often in conformity with religious beliefs (the bride lifted the **veil** from her face to kiss the groom); to hide or conceal (she attempted to **veil** her emotions so her mother wouldn't see how upset she was)

vane/vein/vain (see vain/vane/vein)

veil/vale (see vale/veil)

vein/vain/vane (see vain/vane/vein)

verses/versus

verses: Poems or pieces of poetry or metrical lines in poetry (**verses** are quite distinct from prose); the short divisions of chapters in the Bible (one of the shortest **verses** in the Bible is "Jesus wept")

versus: Against or opposed to (the 2010 Davis Cup resulted in France **versus** Serbia in the finals, with Serbia the eventual winner; the case listed today in the courts is Farley **versus** Farley)

versus/verses (see verses/versus)

vial/vile

vial: A small, usually glass, bottle for liquids (she put a **vial** of smelling salts in her handbag)

vile: Highly offensive or disgusting (there is a **vile** smell coming from that garbage bin; the way he treats his wife makes him a **vile** person)

vile/vial (see vial/vile)

⸃ W ⸂

wade/weighed

wade: To walk through water, sand, swamp, snow, etc. that impedes free movement (Ethan wanted to **wade** through the mud but his mother stopped him); to laboriously move through something (to be prepared for the meeting, the councilor had to **wade** through many complex documents)

weighed: The past tense of "to weigh," meaning to measure the weight of an item by means of a scale, balance, etc. (the dieter was disgusted when the scale showed she **weighed** more than when she started the diet); considered carefully (the judge **weighed** his words carefully before he made his judgment)

wail/whale

wail: A cry of suffering; a lament (there was a **wail** from the child when he lost sight of his mother in the crowd); to cry out in sadness or pain (I put the pacifier in the baby's mouth before she started to **wail**)

whale: The largest of the marine mammals (many sightseers came to watch the female **whale** with her calf as they migrated north); colloquial: to have a great time (we had a **whale of a time** at the festival)

wails/Wales/whales

wails: Plural of "wail," meaning a cry of suffering (the **wails** of the widower could be heard during the funeral); cries out (the baby **wails** when he wants to be fed)

Wales: One of the three countries of Great Britain [i.e., England, Scotland, and **Wales**]

whales: Plural of "whale" (many tourists come to watch the **whales** surface and lift their tails into the air)

waist/waste

waist: The part of the human body between the ribs and the hips (in the 18th century an 18-inch **waist** in a female was considered desirable, and many were laced into corsets to achieve this goal)

waste: To squander, to consume or spend without thought, or to fritter away (I won't **waste** words trying to get him to study for his exams); becoming ill, thin, and frail (she will **waste away** unless she gets medical attention); garbage (please place your **waste** in the cans provided)

wait/weight

wait: To stay in readiness or in expectation (I will **wait** 10 minutes and not a minute longer for him to arrive); to postpone (he has decided to **wait** until the letter arrives rather than phone the doctor for the results); to serve or to attend to someone (the head waiter wanted to **wait** on the important guests himself); to delay going to bed (I will **wait up** until he comes home from the meeting)

weight: How heavy an object is (the **weight** of the package determines the cost to mail it); an oppressive load (the loss of the business and their income is a great **weight** on both of them); importance (what the prime minister says carries a lot of **weight** in the press); to share work fairly (everyone in the group **pulled their weight**)

waive/wave

waive: To relinquish or to forbear (the committee decided to **waive** the entrance fee for seniors to the art exhibition)

wave: The movement of water in a sea, river, lake, etc. in the form of a swell (I knew immediately that the **wave** was too high and I would be dumped on the sand); a swell or rush of emotion (everyone on the lifeboat felt a **wave** of despair when the rescue ship passed them by); a gesture of farewell (she gave a **wave** as she left by ship for Europe)

Wales/whales/wails (see wails/Wales/whales)

want/wont

want: To desire; to feel a need (I **want** to go to the movies); to feel inclined (you can do whatever you **want** to do); to be lacking in or deficient (he was in **want** of money and couldn't pay off his debts); colloquial: to desire to withdraw (if you **want** out of this deal, you only have to let us know)

wont: Accustomed or likely to (he is **wont** to talk a great deal when he has had too much to drink)

war/wore

war: Armed conflict between states or nations (though there have been only two world wars, the world has hardly ever been free of **war**); conflict in general (the couple exchanged a **war** of words in front of their children); colloquial: anger (he is at **war** with the world over the council's indecision)

wore: Past tense of "to wear" (the bride **wore** a beautiful, white wedding gown); overcame (she **wore down** the opposition with her brilliant speech in support of animal liberation); diminished (the effects of the anesthetic **wore off** after a short while)

warn/worn

warn: To advise of likely danger (you need to **warn** the children not to stay out in the sun too long)

worn: Past tense of "to wear," meaning to have on the body as a covering (he has **worn** those same clothes for the past week!); deteriorated (he has **worn** a hole in his sock; the book is **worn** from so much handling)

waste/waist (see waist/waste)

wave/waive (see waive/wave)

wax/whacks

wax: A sticky, yellowish, moldable substance secreted by honeybees as honeycomb; a thick sticky substance often in ears (he needs to go to the doctor to have the **wax** removed from his ears); a polish for furniture or cars (the young boy was observed diligently putting polishing **wax** on his father's car)

whacks: Resounding blows (although not permissible today, years ago many schoolchildren used to receive **whacks** of the cane across their knuckles)

way/weigh/whey

way: The manner or mode (she has a particular **way** of holding her pen); a road, route, etc. (the fastest

way to get to New York from Philadelphia is to drive); progression (he is **on his way** to obtaining a science degree)

weigh: To measure (you need to **weigh** the flour accurately to ensure the dough will rise); to judge the worth of (discerning voters **weigh** the proposals of opposing parties)

whey: The watery part of milk remaining after separation from the curd by coagulation, as in cheese-making (from the famous nursery rhyme: "Little Miss Muffet, sat on a tuffet, eating her curds and **whey**")

weak/week

weak: Lacking strength physically or emotionally (he was so **weak** that he was unable to eat or drink without assistance; she was too **weak** to stand up for herself against her husband's constant abuse); lacking power (our team is too **weak** to beat the leading team); something easily broken (the stand for the new digital television is **weak** and could break); not forceful or convincing (the argument put forward is **weak** and will not convince the doubters to support us); also, to have less substance or intensity [e.g., **weak** tea]

week: A period of seven consecutive days (a **week** can seem a long time when you are waiting to be married)

weather/whether

weather: The atmosphere with regard to wind, temperature, moisture, etc. (the **weather** forecast today is for extremely hot temperatures during the day with a cool night); to dry out or discolor through exposure to the elements (don't leave the tables outside, or they will **weather** and be worthless); colloquial: to withstand (don't worry, we will **weather** this loss and will one day have our own home again)

whether: Used to introduce alternatives (**whether** we go to your place or mine doesn't matter to me); to offer a single alternative with the other implied (would you go and see **whether** it is raining?)

weave/we've

weave: To interlace fibers to form a texture or fabric (Jennifer was well equipped to **weave** at home); to wind through a crowd (to reach their destination they had to **weave** through a number of people waiting to see the fireworks); to include in a story, thesis, etc. (the author's plan was to **weave** the idea of the brother being the murderer throughout the novel)

we've: A contraction of "we have" (**we've** nothing in common, so please don't call me again)

we'd/weed

we'd: A contraction of "we had" or "we would" (**we'd** love to go on vacation with you)

weed: A plant growing wild, especially in cultivated areas (please pull that **weed** before it spreads across the garden)

weed/we'd (see we'd/weed)

week/weak (see weak/week)

weigh/whey/way (see way/weigh/whey)

weighed/wade (see wade/weighed)

weight/wait (see wait/weight)

wen/when

> **wen:** A benign cyst or tumor protruding from under the skin (she was very upset when she noticed the **wen** on her finger)

> **when:** An adverb indicating time (**when** will you have your essay finished? do you remember **when** we last went dancing?)

wet/whet

> **wet:** Dampened by a liquid (our clothes were **wet** after we were caught in a rainstorm); rainy (it has been a very **wet** day); colloquial: young and inexperienced (Ben is **wet behind the ears**)

> **whet:** To sharpen a knife, blade, etc. by friction or grinding (you need to **whet** the carving knife before slicing the Thanksgiving turkey); to be keen, eager (it doesn't take much to **whet** Heather's appetite when you start talking about food)

we've/weave (see weave/we've)

whacks/wax (see wax/whacks)

whale/wail (see wail/whale)

whales/wails/Wales (see wails/Wales/whales)

wheeled/wield

> **wheeled:** Past tense of "to wheel," meaning to propel or to move (he **wheeled** the garbage bin out to the street for collection)

> **wield:** To use or handle a weapon with skill (he can **wield** a sword with great power and accuracy); to exercise power or to dominate (council members are able to **wield** great power in the community)

when/wen (see wen/when)

whet/wet (see wet/whet)

whether/weather (see weather/whether)

whey/way/weigh (see way/weigh/whey)

which/witch

> **which:** Interrogative, asking for selection between this person or persons or thing (**which** shoes should I wear with this suit?); relative pronoun that the article referred to (**which** house do you intend to purchase?); previously referred to (the storm has raged all night, during **which** time the sewage drains have been unable to cope with the extra water)

> **witch:** A female person believed to practice black magic; a sorceress (fairytales usually portray a **witch** with a broomstick and black pointed hat); name used as an insult (I hate you, you ugly, old **witch**!)

while/wile

while: Time given to an action (**while** I am doing my homework, I am not allowed to watch the television); a space of time (we haven't seen the Wilsons for a long **while**)

wile: A trick intended for deceit, used mostly in plural form (she used her **wiles** to trick him into proposing marriage); description of a deceitful person (he is a **wiley** old man, always trying to get you involved in something that only benefits him)

whine/wine

whine: To make a sound or utter words of complaint (you seem to **whine** about everything from politics to the behavior of young people today); to emit a high pitched, monotonous, continuous noise (the annoying **whine** of that machine can be heard all day)

wine: An alcoholic drink made from grapes (do you prefer red or white **wine**?)

whined/wind/wined

whined: Past tense of "to whine" (she **whined** about the weather the whole time we were on vacation)

wind: To coil in rings (it was his task to **wind** the rope around the mooring); to turn or twist (don't forget to **wind** the kitchen timer so we know when the cookies will be done); a bend or turn (this road has a sharp **wind** in it)

whirred/word

whirred: Past tense of "to whir," meaning to move, to revolve, with a vibratory sound (the grasshoppers' wings **whirred** loudly as they flew away when the farmer approached)

word: A unit of language, consisting of one or more spoken sounds or their written representation, that stands alone (a child's first **word** is usually "dada" or "mama"; in grammar a **word** can be a noun, verb, adjective, pronoun, etc); to speak to (I would like a quiet **word** with you about your mother's health); assurance (you need to give me your **word** that you will make that payment tomorrow); colloquial: dependable or trustworthy (he is always **as good as his word** and will certainly come to help you move house); colloquial: to repeat (he told me what he had heard **word for word**); a promise (you have **my word** that I will be there on time)

whoa/woe

whoa: The command to stop or halt (the horse always reacted immediately when its rider said "**whoa, whoa**")

woe: Sorrow, grief, or loss (**woe** is me!)

whole/hole (see hole/whole)

wholly/holey/holy (see holey/holy/wholly)

who's/whose

who's: A contraction of "who is" (**who's** coming with me to the art gallery?)

whose: An interrogative pronoun (**whose** shoes made those marks on the clean floor?)

whose/who's (see who's/whose)

wield/wheeled (see wheeled/wield)

wile/while (see while/wile)

wind/whined (see whined/wind)

wine/whine (see whine/wine)

witch/which (see which/witch)

woe/whoa (see whoa/woe)

won/one (see one/won)

wont/want (see want/wont)

wood/would

wood: Timber (I particularly like walnut or maple **wood**; could you pick up the pieces of **wood** over there for the fire?); a golf club, also called a driver (do you need a **wood** or an iron for this shot?)

would: Indicating a desire or intention (I **would** like to go to the movies next week); conditionally (**would** you want to fly to Europe now with the likelihood of the volcano erupting in Iceland?); to make a less blunt statement (to spend all that money on yourself **would** hardly be fair) word/whirred (see whirred/word)

wore/war (see war/wore)

worn/warn (see warn/worn)

would/wood (see wood/would)

wrap/rap (see rap/wrap)

wrapped/rapped/rapt (see rapped/rapt/wrapped)

wreak/reek (see reek/wreak)

wrest/rest (see rest/wrest)

wretch/retch (see retch/wretch)

wring/ring (see ring/wring)

write/right/rite (see right/rite/write)

wrote/rote (see rote/wrote)

wrung/rung (see rung/wrung)

wry/rye (see rye/wry)

⋛ Y ⋚

yew/you/ewe (see ewe/yew/you)

yews/ewes/use (see ewes/use/yews)

yoke/yolk

yoke: A device for joining together a pair of draft animals, especially oxen, usually consisting of a crosspiece with two bow-shaped pieces each enclosing the head of an animal (it is quite common to see oxen in a **yoke** pulling a heavy cart on farms); the top fitted piece of a garment (she embroidered small pink flowers on the **yoke** of her nightdress); to join or unite together (we need to **yoke** the animals before we start ploughing the field)

yolk: The yellow part in the center of an egg (I like the **yolk** to be very soft when I have poached eggs for breakfast)

yolk/yoke (see yoke/yolk)

yore/your/you're

yore: Times past (it was a common expression to talk of "in days of **yore**," meaning many years ago)

your: A possessive pronoun meaning something that belongs to you or a group (be careful of **your** language in front of **your** grandmother)

you're: A contraction of "you are" (it is a pity **you're** not able to attend the wedding)

you/ewe/yew (see ewe/yew/you)

you'll/Yule

you'll: A contraction of "you will" (**you'll** want to take your umbrella with you because the forecast calls for rain)

Yule: Christmas or the Christmas season (**Yule**tide greetings are often written on Christmas cards)

your/you're/yore (see yore/your/you're)

you're/yore/your (see yore/your/you're)

Yule/you'll (see you'll/Yule)

yon

gait

right

gale

whether

pedal

write

ewe

weather

faint

revue

review

later

disinterested

peddle

faint

emigrant

warn

all

thrown

latter

awl

immigrant

mistrust

uninterested

distrust

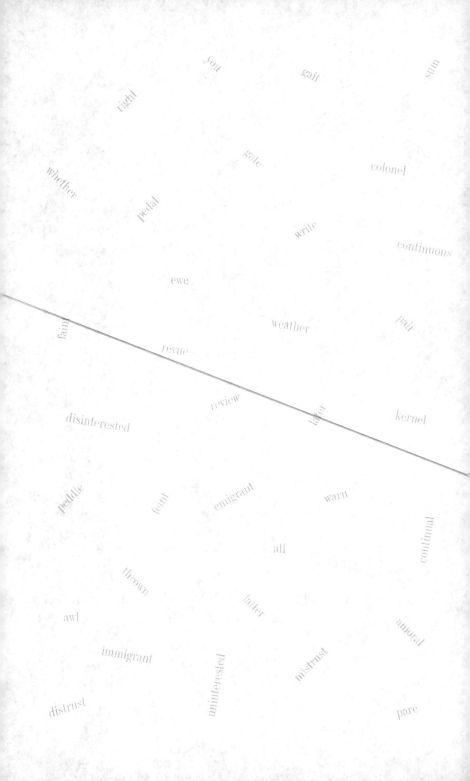

accept/except

accept: To take willingly something that has been offered (it is with great pleasure that I **accept** your invitation to present the prizes at the graduation ceremony); to agree to or admit responsibility (we will **accept** the student's version of events when we receive confirmation; we **accept** that we have a duty to ensure that our employees are paid); to concede (I will have to **accept** that you are a better sportsman than I am)

except: To exclude or leave out (we can all go to the movies **except** Jeremy, as he has the measles)

adverse/averse

adverse: Contrary or antagonistic (the **adverse** weather made us reconsider our plans for a picnic; they could never agree, because their opinions were so **adverse**)

averse: To be disinclined (she was **averse** to leaving the party so early)

advice/advise

advice: A recommendation or opinion (I will take your **advice** and walk the scenic route)

advise: To offer an opinion or counsel (I **advise** you to go home and get some sleep)

affect/effect

affect: To act on or produce a change (cancer can **affect** many organs in the body); to pretend or imitate (to **affect** an upper-class accent)

effect: A result or accomplishment (our relationship should have no **effect** on my family; the ruling had no **effect** in reducing the disturbances)

afflicted/inflicted

afflicted: Distress with mental or bodily pain (he was **afflicted** by polio at a very young age)

inflicted: Imposed punishment, additional duties, or similar (the father **inflicted** punishment on the child for refusing to eat his dinner)

aggravate/irritate (now widely used interchangeably)

aggravate: To make worse or intensify (you will only **aggravate** the wound if you continue to pull at the bandage)

irritate: To anger or annoy (Paul's continual interruptions were a deliberate attempt to **irritate** the speaker)

allegiance/alliance

allegiance: Loyalty to a sovereign, country, or government, or to a cause (he pledged his **allegiance** to the flag and his country)

alliance: A union of countries, businesses, trade associations, etc. for mutual benefit (the Triple **Alliance** of Germany, Austria–Hungary, and Italy was formed in 1882 for mutual support against other European powers; trade unions formed an **alliance** to protest against the government's wage cuts)

all together/altogether

all together: As a group (when we are **all together**, we usually have a great time)

altogether: Entirely or completely (that was **altogether** the worst experience I have ever had); on the whole (**altogether**, we were lucky to escape the storm); in all (the restaurant bill **altogether** came to $100)

allude/elude

allude: To refer to casually (notice how many times Sarah will **allude** to her successful parents); to contain an indirect reference to something already known (this report **alludes** to the lack of input from the public)

elude: To escape skillfully or avoid (he was able to **elude** the police by posing as a paramedic); to forget (his name is one of those names that always seems to **elude** me)

alternate/alternative

alternate: To do things in turn (we will **alternate** the position of deputy mayor every two months); to follow (day and night **alternate** with each other)

alternative: The offering of a choice (the **alternative** to going to bed without your dinner is to eat everything that is on your plate; you have an **alternative**: either agree with what is being said or vote with the opposition)

ambiguous/ambivalent

ambiguous: Obscure, vague, capable of different interpretations (in the interview, Jennifer queried the question asked, as it was **ambiguous**)

ambivalent: To hold two conflicting opinions or emotions at the same time (Peter was **ambivalent** about the boat refugees' situation)

amoral/immoral

amoral: Lacking a moral sense or standards; not caring about or aware of what is right or wrong (it was **amoral** for people to raise money to help those suffering from the floods and then to keep for themselves a large amount of the funds collected)

immoral: Not conforming to a given set of standards or accepted patterns of behavior (in some countries adultery is considered **immoral** and the female can be stoned to death)

appraise/apprise

appraise: To assess the worth of something (we **appraise** the value of this horse at $2,000)

apprise: To inform (you should **apprise** the government of the situation in Japan immediately)

biannual/biennial

biannual: Occurring twice a year (our **biannual** fair is held every year in January and July)

biennial: Happening every two years (the **biennial** festival is scheduled next year in November)

ceremonial/ceremonious

ceremonial: Relating to formalities observed at solemn or important occasions (the **ceremonial** rites of baptism were observed with the child being sprinkled with water)

ceremonious: Excessively formal or polite (the usher was **ceremonious** in the way he showed us to our seats and made sure we were comfortable)

childish/childlike

childish: Acting like a child; weak, silly (it always annoys me when Peter plays these silly games and is so **childish**)

childlike: To have the qualities of a child (her artistic works are so **childlike**)

complementary/complimentary

complementary: Something that completes or balances to make a whole (the violins, viola, and cello are **complementary** parts of a string quartet)

complimentary: Something given away for free (we received **complimentary** tickets for the ballet); expressing a compliment (the critic made **complimentary** remarks when reviewing the play)

confidant/confident

confidant: Someone to whom secrets are confided (Jack has been my **confidant** for many years, as I can depend on him not to reveal anything I tell him); the feminine of confidant is confidante

confident: Believing in your abilities; being sure of yourself (Jimmy was **confident** that he would win the title bout; the Republican Party is **confident** of victory in the coming elections)

conscience/conscious

conscience: The internal mechanism that allows a person to distinguish right from wrong and act accordingly (Carl wrestled with his **conscience** and finally made the decision to tell the truth about taking the money left on the table)

conscious: Aware of and responding to one's feelings, own existence, surroundings, etc. (Rebecca was **conscious** of her feelings of inadequacy when dealing with the attempted suicide of her brother)

consequently/subsequently

consequently: As a result of a previous action (I forgot to take my umbrella with me when I went for a walk and **consequently** was soaked when it started to rain)

subsequently: Following closely in time, order, or sequence (we were late arriving at the movie theatre and **subsequently** missed the beginning of the film)

continual/continuous

continual: Proceedings continuing over some time but with periods of interruption (the **continual** interjections during the president's speech were irritating to all who attended the rally; the mother was annoyed by her children's **continual** interruptions while she was making dinner)

continuous: Proceedings extending over time without interruption (there was a **continuous** procession of cars following the hearse to the cemetery)

defective/deficient

defective: Being faulty or imperfect (Susie returned the new kettle to the store where she purchased it as it was **defective** and had a missing part)

deficient: Lacking some element or quality: inadequate (the mother thought her daughter was totally **deficient** in common sense when she went shopping without the list of groceries)

detract/distract

detract: To take away (as you did not turn up for work until 9:30 this morning, I will **detract** one hour's pay from your wages); to reduce in quality, value, or status (please don't wear that pink blouse, because it will **detract** from the rest of your outfit)

distract: To divert the mind or attention (keep him busy and **distract** his attention until I have finished making this model for his birthday)

diminish/minimize

diminish: To reduce, decrease, or lessen (it has been raining heavily but, according to the forecast, it should **diminish** to just a few showers soon)

minimize: To lessen to the smallest possible amount or degree (you will need to **minimize** the dosage of medicine you are taking until it is reduced to just half a teaspoon a day)

disinformation/misinformation

disinformation: Misleading information given intentionally (during the Cold War, both the communists and the free world provided **disinformation** to confuse their opponents and to assist their own cause)

misinformation: Information that is misleading but not intentionally (the **misinformation** regarding the museum's opening times was given by the girl at the information desk)

disinterested/uninterested

disinterested: Unbiased, objective, or impartial (as a **disinterested** witness he was able to give an unbiased view of what had happened)

uninterested: Indifferent; lacking interest (he was **uninterested** in the conversation between his brother and his girlfriend)

displaced/misplaced

displaced: Shifted from its original place, particularly with regard to people (many survivors of World War II became **displaced** persons when they could not return to their homes); removed from office and be replaced (he was **displaced** as the chairman and replaced by his deputy when the profits of the company went into sharp decline)

misplaced: Put in the wrong place (Isabel searched everywhere for her car keys, which she had obviously **misplaced**, and eventually found them in the jacket she had worn the day before)

distrust/mistrust

distrust: Regard with doubt or suspicion (I **distrust** the way he handles the accounts for the business)

mistrust: Lack of trust or confidence (her mother and father **mistrust** the lavish attention given to their daughter by her boyfriend)

elicit/illicit

elicit: To extract or bring out (we need to **elicit** more information before we decide to pursue this case)

illicit: Illegal or not allowed (**illicit** drugs have been smuggled into this country on boats and airplanes)

eminent/imminent

eminent: Distinguished: of high repute (the population mourned when the **eminent** brain surgeon was murdered in an attempted robbery); noteworthy or remarkable (the residents and the government acknowledged the **eminent** services of the firefighters during the brush fires)

imminent: Likely to occur at any moment (the information coming from all sources indicated that war in the Middle East was **imminent**)

emigrant/immigrant

emigrant: A person who leaves one country to settle in another (Peter was an **emigrant** when he left England to migrate to Australia)

immigrant: A person who comes into a country to settle (Peter was an **immigrant** when he arrived in his new country of Australia)

empathy/sympathy

empathy: Being able to feel and share the emotions that someone else is experiencing (having lost her children in the floods, Sara had **empathy** for the parents whose children were killed in the bus crash)

sympathy: Feeling compassion and concern but not actually sharing the emotions (Ken expressed his **sympathy** in a letter to his friend when he read of his father's death in the obituaries)

eventually/ultimately

eventually: An unspecified time in the future (you will understand **eventually** why it was necessary for us to leave our country)

ultimately: Finally; at the end (**ultimately**, you alone are responsible for your actions)

everyday/every day

everyday: An adjective referring to something that happens daily or is commonplace (it is an **everyday** occurrence for Katie to say she is too sick to go to school)

every day: Each day (you need to check your briefcase **every day** before you go to work)

explicit/implicit

explicit: Clearly expressed, nothing implied (he was quite **explicit** that his intention is to leave his job at the end of the month)

implicit: A statement or view implied or suggested but not expressly stated (it was **implicit** in his comments that he did not like my friend's attitude regarding taking drugs); unquestioning or unreserved (he had **implicit** confidence in his friend's ability to handle the situation)

fewer/less

fewer: Used to indicate smaller numbers of people or things (we had **fewer** people nominated for positions on the council than last time)

less: Smaller in size or quantity (Andrew received **less** food on his plate than his brother)

forego/forgo

forego: To go before; to precede

forgo: To abstain from doing something or to do without (Ken decided to **forgo** his lunch to make certain he would not be late for the meeting)

imply/infer

imply: To suggest without stating explicitly: to hint (the politician seemed to **imply** that he was going to run for re-election)

infer: To draw a conclusion from (can I **infer** from what you just said that you intend to take action on the high numbers of underage drinkers?)

later/latter

later: Occurring or coming after the due or expected time (I will leave a key under the mat for you in case you get here **later** than 11, when I go to bed)

latter: The second of two options (I will accept the **latter** of the two choices you have given me); toward the end (the chapter you are referring to is in the **latter** part of the book)

mediate/mitigate

mediate: To bring about an agreement between disagreeing parties (the court appointed an arbitrator to **mediate** a financial settlement between the two parties)

mitigate: To lessen in force or intensity (he was able to **mitigate** the pain by taking strong painkillers and remaining still; they could do nothing to **mitigate** the force of the wind and watched helplessly as a tree fell on their house)

overdo/overdue

overdo: To carry to excess; to exaggerate or overreact (you always **overdo** everything, but that isn't a criticism); to exert more than your strength (don't **overdo** the lifting, or you might get a hernia)

overdue: Past the due time; late (the bank has advised that our monthly repayment wasn't made on the due date and is now **overdue**)

persecute/prosecute

persecute: To harass, torment, or cause suffering, often because of a perceived injustice or as a result of adherence to different religious beliefs or principles (it has been common practice over the centuries for religious institutions to **persecute** those whose beliefs are different from their own)

prosecute: To institute or carry out legal proceedings against an individual, company, etc. for an alleged crime or wrongdoing (the council decided to **prosecute** the owner of a noisy establishment after many complaints from nearby residents)

prescribe/proscribe

prescribe: To lay down in writing a rule or a course of action that must be followed (the school will **prescribe** a list of books for summer reading); in medicine, to designate a course of action (the doctor will **prescribe** the correct medication for your condition)

proscribe: To condemn or prohibit (the court has deemed it necessary to **proscribe** the keeping of certain breeds of dogs that are considered dangerous to humans)

regretfully/regrettably

regretfully: Expressing sorrow or loss over something (**regretfully,** I will not be able to attend the funeral of our dear friend on Friday)

regrettably: To feel sorry or disappointed about something (**regrettably,** there has been a breakdown on the highway and you will have to wait here until the situation has been resolved)

wreak/wreck

wreak: To inflict or execute (he was determined to **wreak** vengeance for the murder of his sister); to cause a large amount of damage or harm (they were aware that a tsunami could **wreak** havoc on the seaside towns and built large walls as protection)

wreck: The destruction, ruin of cars, buildings, ships, etc. (after the accident, our car was a complete **wreck** and was written off by the insurance company); colloquial: the visible effects on humans of physical suffering, disease, etc. (Simon was a total **wreck** after losing his business during the financial crisis)

you

gait

right

gate

whether

pedal

write

ewe

faint

weather

revue

review

later

disinterested

peddle

feint

emigrant

warn

all

thrown

latter

awl

immigrant

uninterested

mistrust

distrust

WORDS OFTEN MISSPELLED

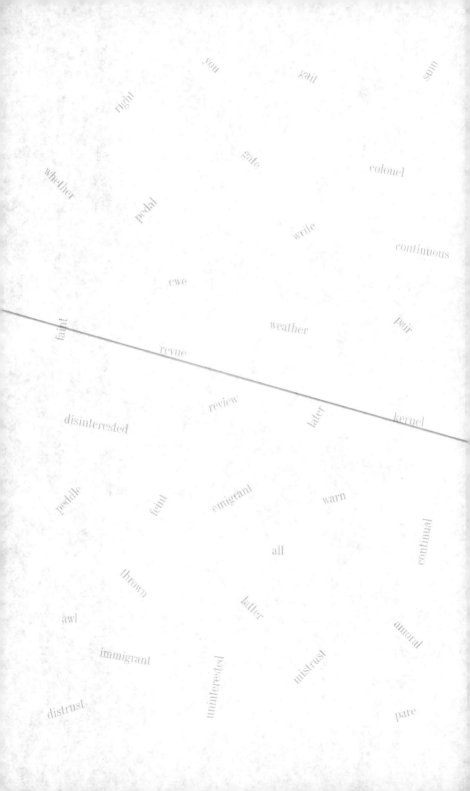

you

gait

sum

right

gate

colonel

whether

pedal

write

continuous

ewe

faint

weather

pair

revue

review

later

kernel

disinterested

peddle

feint

emigrant

warn

all

continual

thrown

latter

awl

amoral

immigrant

uninterested

mistrust

distrust

pare

≳ A ≲

Absence

Acceptable

Accessible

Accidental

Accommodate/
accommodation

Achieved

Acknowledge

Acquainted

Acquiesce/acquiescence

Acquire

Addresses

Advertise

Aerial

Aggravate

Aggregate

Agreeable

A lot

Amateur

Analysis

Ancillary

Appall/appalled

Apparent

Appearance

Argument

Arrangement

Ascend

Assessment

Automation

≳ B ≲

Beginning

Believe

Beneficial

Benefited

Bias

Briefly

Budgeted

≳ C ≲

Calendar

Category

Ceiling

Celsius

Cemetery

Changeable

Chaos

Chaotic

Citizen

Colleague

Column

Committed

Comparative

Compatible

Competition

Connoisseur

Conscience

Conscientious

Conscious

Consensus

Convenience

Corroborate

Courteous

Courtesy

Criticism

Cursory

⋛ D ⋚

Dais

Deceive

Decision

Deficient

Definitely

Desirable

Desperate

Dilemma

Disappoint

Discipline

Discrepancy

Dispel

Dissatisfied

Distributor

⋛ E ⋚

Efficiency

Embarrass/embarrassed

Environment

Erroneous

Especially

Essential

Exaggerate

Except

Exercise

Exhilarate

Existence

Explanation

Extremely

﹥ F ﹤

Fahrenheit
Familiar
Fascinating
Feasible
Fiery
Financial
Foreign
Fulfill

﹥ G ﹤

Gauge
Government
Granddaughter
Grateful
Grievance
Guarantee
Guard
Guardian

﹥ H ﹤

Harass
Height
Heroes
Humorous

﹥ I ﹤

Immediate
Independent
Indispensable
Interfere
Interpretation
Irrelevant
Irreparable
Irritable

﹥ J ﹤

Judgment

﹥ K ﹤

Knowledge
Knowledgeable

﹥ L ﹤

Leisure
Liaison
License

﹥ M ﹤

Maintenance
Maneuver
Masquerade
Medieval

Memento

Millennium

Miniature

Miniscule

Mischievous

Misspell

≥ N ≤

Naïve

Nausea

Necessary

Negotiate

Niece

Neighbor

Noticeable

≥ O ≤

Occasionally

Occurrence

Omission

Omitted

≥ P ≤

Parallel

Pastime

Perseverance

Personnel

Persuade

Physiology

Playwright

Possess

Preceding

Preference

Prejudice

Preliminary

Privilege

Procedure

Professor

Pronunciation

Proprietary

Psychology

Publicly

≥ Q ≤

Questionnaire

Quintessential

≥ R ≤

Receipt

Receive

Recommend

Reference

Regrettable
Relief
Relieved
Relinquish
Renege
Replaceable
Rhyme
Rhythm

≳ S ≲

Scarcely
Schedule
Secretary
Separate
Similar
Sincerely
Statutory
Successfully
Supersede
Synonymous

≳ T ≲

Tariff
Temporary
Tendency
Tomato/tomatoes
Transfer/transferred
Twelfth

≳ U ≲

Underrate
Undoubtedly
Unnecessary
Usually

≳ V ≲

Vacuum
Valuable

≳ W ≲

Weird
Withhold

REFERENCES

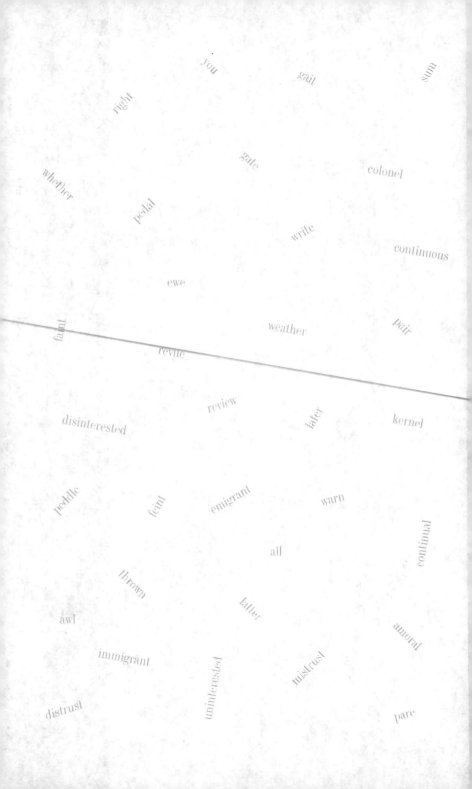

The Concise Oxford Dictionary of Current English, 11th edition (London: Oxford University Press, London, 2008).

Merriam-Webster's Collegiate Dictionary, 11th edition (Merriam-Webster, Inc., 2003).

New Oxford American Dictionary, 3rd edition (New York: Oxford University Press, 2010).

The Oxford Paperback Dictionary (London: Oxford University Press, 1979).

Rothwell, David. *Dictionary of Homonyms* (Hertfordshire, UK: Wordsworth Editions Limited, 2007).

Webster's New World Student's Dictionary, Revised Edition (New York: Hungry Minds, Inc., 1996).

you

gait

right

gate

whether

pedal

write

ewe

faint

weather

revue

review

later

disinterested

peddle

feint

emigrant

warn

all

thrown

latter

awl

immigrant

mistrust

uninterested

distrust

you   gait   sum

right

gate   colonel

whether

pedal   write   continuous

ewe

faint   weather   pair

revue

review   later   kernel

disinterested

peddle   feint   emigrant   warn

all   continual

thrown

latter

awl   amoral

immigrant   uninterested   mistrust

distrust   pare

ELIZABETH MORRISON has a BA DipEd (Dist) from the University of Newcastle. She started as a history teacher in the School of General Studies, progressing to head teacher and senior head teacher of humanities, and later Head of Branch. A freelance journalist for many years, Elizabeth also taught professional and media writing in the School of Communications of Charles Sturt University.